Exploring
Safely

A Guide for
Elementary
Teachers

Exploring Safely

A Guide for Elementary Teachers

By Terry Kwan and Juliana Texley

NATIONAL SCIENCE TEACHERS ASSOCIATION

Arlington, Virginia

NATIONAL SCIENCE TEACHERS ASSOCIATION

Claire Reinburg, Director
Judy Cusick, Associate Editor
Carol Duval, Associate Editor
Betty Smith, Associate Editor

ART AND DESIGN Linda Olliver, Director
    Shennen Bersani, Cover Illustration
    Linda Olliver, Inside Illustration
NSTA WEB Tim Weber, Webmaster
PERIODICALS PUBLISHING Shelley Carey, Director
PRINTING AND PRODUCTION Catherine Lorrain-Hale, Director
    Nguyet Tran, Assistant Production Manager
    Jack Parker, Desktop Publishing Specialist
PUBLICATIONS OPERATIONS Erin Miller, Manager
*sci*LINKS Tyson Brown, Manager

NATIONAL SCIENCE TEACHERS ASSOCIATION
Gerald F. Wheeler, Executive Director
David Beacom, Publisher

SC*I*INKS.
THE WORLD'S A CLICK AWAY

Featuring sciLINKS®—a new way of connecting text and the Internet. Up-to-the-minute online content, classroom ideas, and other materials are just a click away. Go to page viii to learn more about this new educational resource.

Exploring Safely: *A Guide for Elementary Teachers*
    NSTA Stock Number: PB166X1
    ISBN: 0-87355-200-8
    Library of Congress Control Number: 2001098898
    Printed in Canada by Webcom
    Printed on recycled paper

NSTA PRESS
    1840 Wilson Boulevard
    Arlington, Virginia 22201-3000
    www.nsta.org

NSTA is committed to publishing quality materials that promote the best in inquiry-based science education. However, conditions of actual use may vary and the safety procedures and practices described in this book are intended to serve only as a guide. Additional precautionary measures may be required. NSTA and the author(s) do not warrant or represent that the procedures and practices in this book meet any safety code or standard or federal, state, or local regulations. NSTA and the author(s) disclaim any liability for personal injury or damage to property arising out of or relating to the use of this book including any of the recommendations, instructions, or materials contained therein.

Contents

Preface

It has been many years since NSTA released a laboratory safety guide for teachers. In that time, many things have changed. We have more to teach—and the concepts are more complex. High-stakes tests have narrowed our focus and sharpened the scrutiny of our communities. Technology has permitted us to gather and transmit information with increasing speed; it has also allowed us to make lab experiences more like real-world science.

Social conditions have changed too. Today's teachers work with increasingly diverse student populations, including students with many special needs and sensitivities for whom they must design lab and field work. The public is more litigious, increasing teachers' concerns about liability. We also know more about potential hazards. We have access to new research and data about toxicity of materials and dangers in methods that were not apparent years ago.

But today's students need hands-on experience in science more than ever. They need to observe and investigate, practicing the skills that will enable them to make good decisions and to work in the complex world of the 21st century.

The good news is that we now have information about alternatives and options that we never had before. We can still provide the investigative and observational activities that are essential to helping students understand the content and the methods of science. We can still set the scene for the discrepant events that produce the "Aha!" so essential to engendering true understanding and love of the scientific endeavor. Teachers today can implement exciting curricula based on the National Science Education Standards in a safe learning environment if they have background knowledge and good sense. To do so requires planning and preparation, but it's well worth the effort.

This book is intended to offer positive options, even as it raises awareness of potential hazards. *Exploring Safely* is the elementary edition, followed by *Inquiring Safely* for middle school teachers, and *Investigating Safely* for high school teachers. While we've included many anecdotes—all true stories, except for the names—from the designated grade ranges, the general principles are the same.

This elementary volume is for both self-contained classroom teachers and science specialists. It also has many applications for administrators and central office personnel. Be sure to share it as needed, so that your entire school community will become more conscious of safety.

While the traditional safety manual tends to be a compilation of safety rules, regulations, and lists, this book takes another path. We offer a more narrative style, providing discussions of safety concepts in the context of commonplace situations in real classrooms. We hope this approach makes these books enjoyable to read as well as to reference.

We also hope that the books are thought provoking. No single publication can cover every eventuality. We encourage you to make connections and generalize from the ideas presented. Our goal is to provide you, the teacher, with examples of safe practices and to help you become more alert to ways of ensuring safety when you teach science in your classroom and in field studies. Above all, we encourage you to use common sense.

We believe that creating a safe environment for teaching and learning science is a group endeavor, led by the teacher, but joined by the entire school community. As you read this book, we hope it helps you "see" your physical environment and your procedures through a safety-conscious lens. In so doing, you will be able to give your students habits of mind that will last a lifetime.

Special thanks to the contributors who reviewed and added to this document: Kenneth Roy, chair of NSTA's Science Safety Advisory Board; Bob Davis, chair of the Council of State Science Supervisors Writing Committee for Science and Safety; Eric Pyle, chair of NSTA's Special Education Advisory Board; Fran Hess; Judy Williams; Sandra West; Gloria Rudisch, M.D.; Tim Champion; Lance Rudiger; Janice Danielson; and Sue Senator. Their tireless work has helped us polish our view of the classroom and enrich our offerings to you, the teacher.

Author Biographies

Terry Kwan taught middle and high school science before becoming a science supervisor and independent contractor, collaborating with private and public institutions to develop science programs, train teachers, and design science facilities. She has been a school board member in Brookline, Massachusetts, since 1985 and a community representative to Institutional Biosafety Committees for the Harvard Medical School and the Dana Farber Cancer Institute.

Juliana Texley has taught all the sciences, K to 12, for 25 years and spent 9 as a school superintendent. She was editor of the *Science Teacher* for 12 years and an officer of the Association of Presidential Awardees in Science Teaching. She currently teaches college biology and technology, and develops online curricula for students and teachers.

About the Cover Artist

Shennon Bersani used her daughter Kerrin as the model for this cover. Her continuous curiosity and love of nature made her the perfect choice. Other live models, the goldfish, where taken from Shennon's backyard pond — a haven for birds, butterflies, turtles, frogs, and a ribbon snake. Two colored-pencil illustrations were created, one of Kerrin with the background and one of the bowl of fish. Merging the two on the computer using Photoshop achieved the final image.

Exploring Safely brings you *sci*LINKS, a new project that blends the two main delivery systems for curriculum—books and telecommunications—into a dynamic new educational tool for children, their parents, and their teachers. *sci*LINKS links specific science content with instructionally rich Internet resources. *sci*LINKS represents an enormous opportunity to create new pathways for learners, new opportunities for professional growth among teachers, and new modes of engagement for parents.

In this *sci*LINKed text, you will find an icon near several of the concepts being discussed. Under it, you will find the *sci*LINKS URL (*www.scilinks.org*) and a code. Go to the *sci*LINKS website, sign in, type the code from your text, and you will receive a list of URLs that are selected by science educators. Sites are chosen for accurate and age-appropriate content and good pedagogy. The underlying database changes constantly, eliminating dead or revised sites or simply replacing them with better selections. The *sci*LINKS search team regularly reviews the materials to which this text points, so you can always count on good content being available.

The selection process involves four review stages:

1. First, a cadre of undergraduate science education majors searches the World Wide Web for interesting science resources. The undergraduates submit about 500 sites a week for consideration.

2. Next, packets of these web pages are organized and sent to teacher-webwatchers with expertise in given fields and grade levels. The teacher-webwatchers can also submit web pages that they have found on their own. The teachers pick the jewels from this selection and correlate them to the National Science Education Standards. These pages are submitted to the *sci*LINKS database.

3. Scientists review these correlated sites for accuracy.

4. NSTA staff approve the web pages and edit the information provided for accuracy and consistent style.

*sci*LINKS is a free service for textbook and supplemental resource users, but obviously someone must pay for it. Participating publishers pay a fee to NSTA for each book that contains *sci*LINKS. The program is also supported by a grant from the National Aeronautics and Space Administration (NASA).

Setting the Scene

> Ms. J. has an average third grade—many students, much diversity. But their science skills shine even when she's not around. When the substitute is in, Tetsuko, who speaks only Japanese, takes responsibility for the aquarium. Maria, who is learning disabled, manages the seed experiment. Jean knows where to find the custodian when the class needs more soap for hygiene. Matt makes sure everything is in its place at the end of the day. Ms. J.'s class is a science team, learning together.

Share the Adventure *and* the Responsibility

Investigative science provides the opportunity for students to learn new skills. But it also means more work and responsibility for everyone. An active science program requires the distribution, use, and care of much more material and equipment than a textbook/workbook program. Classroom management is the first key to a safe learning environment—and to satisfaction for the teacher.

The first steps to hands-on science should be small ones. Practice the rules of investigation in short tasks before you try complex ones. At least some of your students may not have had the opportunity to experiment in class before and may perceive activity time as free time. Plan a five-minute investigation with a written response. If that is successful, try a ten-minute project with only a few pieces of equipment to manage. A rule of thumb in education is that children can't concentrate for more minutes than their age in years—about ten minutes for a fourth grader. But you can extend this by including time throughout the activity to respond, write, or assess.

If you try to do all the setup and cleanup yourself, you will find yourself with too little time and too much responsibility. Giving your students the skills to help maintain good organization will not only prevent accidents but will also teach them what they need to conduct their own research in the future. It can also improve class dynamics. Working with real objects and observing cause and effect firsthand often changes the playing field, creating new leaders in class work and challenging students who are great readers but who need help from others to complete an investigative laboratory task. Students who have trouble with reading or math skills may shine at managing materials or may display undiscovered observational and manipulative skills.

The science activity lesson provides an ideal opportunity to teach kids to take responsibility for their actions and their equipment. And for young children, figuring out how many items are needed, counting them as they are distributed, and recounting as they put them away are also ways to practice math skills. If you use a task board for student jobs, be sure to include science supply and equipment jobs. Older students can create diagrams of supply cabinets to make it easy for anyone to understand the system.

Cleanliness and Order— Foundations of Safe Practice

Most kids have seen the movie *The Nutty Professor*. However, the stereotype of the frizzy-haired scientist in the messy lab isn't one we want to perpetuate. Neatness and organization are essential to science. Everything in a science classroom should have a specific place. Safety equipment should be located where it can be quickly and easily grabbed for emergency use. Equipment and furniture should never obstruct escape routes.

The less "stuff" on the work surface, the less likely things will spill or get spilled upon. If a science experiment is to be conducted at a particular table or at student desks, then the surface should be cleared of everything except the equipment and supplies needed for the activity. In particular, food and food containers should not be anywhere near the spaces intended for science experiments. (See Chapter 10.) The less clutter around the work area, the lower the trip/fall hazard. Where to put the backpacks, extra notebooks, and other clutter? Certainly not on the floor next to the work area! In a spill or fire, an escaping student might trip and fall. Try the hall or put a sign on your door reminding students, "No books today."

What students should NOT do:

- Work in a chemical storage room or with stock bottles of chemicals
- Handle new or exotic organisms
- Go on errands without staff supervision
- Transport heavy equipment (such as televisions on carts)
- Use strong cleaning compounds or disinfectants

Extra clothing also can pose safety hazards. Those coats and hats can absorb chemicals or catch fire. If items are hung over the backs of students' chairs, the extra weight can cause them to tip over when students stand up or push their chairs away from their tables. Be sure there is a place to hang or store those jackets, caps, and other items that students wear to school but don't need during class time. (See Chapter 10, **Dress of the Day**.)

The Best-Laid Plans

Lesson plans often have great continuity but fall short in the real world. Every day there is someone absent in almost every classroom. That means that your safety precautions must consider the consequences of both teacher and student absences.

Remember that you are responsible for the program offered by your substitute. Because the substitute is unlikely to have your knowledge of the subject matter or the same level of classroom control, it is usually not a good idea to have them conduct complex activities or those with potential hazards. (If you direct them to do so, you could be liable. See Chapter 11.) Many teachers have a special substitute folder for one-day unexpected absences containing safe activities that would fit almost any part of the year. Make sure your substitute has a list of special needs students and the accommodations they require. If you will be absent for an extended period, take time to speak to your substitutes and ensure that they have the competencies to carry out your plans.

When students are absent, they often miss safety directions, so it is important to have a written version and to begin every class with a short review. Be sure that all your safety lessons and directions are included in your lesson plan book. Try to avoid having students out seeing the counselor, special education consultant, or speech therapist during direction time. A student who reenters the room in the middle of a science experience can be a real hazard to the rest of the group.

Students who are absent often need access to the supplies the next day. To save your sanity, you may want to organize these supplies in labeled boxes containing all the supplies for a particular unit. Place a laminated card with the relevant safety rules in the box with the supplies. While clear or translucent containers are ideal, shoeboxes and the ten-ream copy-paper cartons may also serve you well. Create outside labels that show not only the title of the activity, but also a list of the items inside. (See Chapter 4 for storage tips.) Many teachers find that assigning students homework buddies or makeup-work buddies works well.

Following any science activity, the work surface should be washed and dried completely before going on to the next activity. This is a great habit to instill—even if sometimes it doesn't seem necessary. Students can help here, but use only mild dish detergent. You will need a Material Safety Data Sheet (MSDS) for that product. (See Chapter 4.) Don't allow students to leave to see special personnel in the middle of the lab without their own, personal cleanup time.

In a heterogeneous classroom, with many absentees and special needs students, these guidelines may seem daunting. The key—teach responsibility along with science. Every student should feel responsible for every other member of his or her science team every day.

1 The Teachable Moment

Many books begin with a general chapter on safety. While this may be prudent, it doesn't mean much to students when it is abstract. Like everything else we do, safety lessons are best remembered when they are associated with real experiences. Though you may want to review and to post some general safety rules (e.g., hand washing rules and use of safety glasses) right from the start, the best time to give specific safety instruction is in conjunction with a lesson or activity where the safety procedure is needed. And even though the procedure is one you may have reviewed a number of times, do it again every time the activity you have planned requires the precaution.

Following the introduction of a new safety procedure, you might schedule a writing activity in which your students write a story involving the new procedure or an art activity that has students creating the signs and posters to remind themselves of the new safety idea. This provides for good, authentic assessment. Give students the challenge of placing the safety reminder signs and stories near the place where activities call for the reminders. For example, put hand washing signs near live animal cages, and safety–glass reminders near centers where chemicals are to be used. You'll also know they've mastered safety concepts when they can share them with visitors, new students, and returning absentees.

Homework Happens

Many of the safe practices that you promote in science activities can be extended easily to things that take place in students' homes. Reading labels carefully, the safe handling of sharp instruments and glassware, hand washing and cleanup—all have practical applications in the typical kitchen or bathroom. When you give instructions to keep students safe during field studies, these rules will probably keep kids safe when traveling with their parents. So take the opportunity and invite your students to think of how a rule you have just taught them would apply equally well to a situation at home. Help children to think safety wherever they are and whatever they are doing. Encourage them to work with parents to create a child-safe home, especially if younger siblings are present. Every new application of the ideas you present will help reinforce them and make safety a habit rather than an add-on.

You are responsible—and can be held liable—for assignments you give as homework. Consider these carefully. Don't ask students to explore chemicals in their home cabinets without their parents or to test soils in unknown neighborhoods unless you are sure they are safe. But at the same time, don't hesitate to develop safe home assignments for students to share with parents. Many teachers have created portable science kits (backpacks or boxes) that students can check out with such things as plastic thermometers or thermistors, measuring tools, binoculars and star charts, or leaf presses. Parents appreciate these opportunities for interaction, and once families have explored together, they are likely to continue.

Use your newsletter to communicate what you are doing and what your safety precautions are. If your school has an Internet site or a homework hotline, make sure that safety concepts are included. Many teachers also develop a safety contract with their students and have parents read it aloud and review it at home early in the year. It's a good idea to update and repeat the contract process each quarter.

SAFETY CONTRACT

I am learning to be a good scientist. I know that I must be organized, neat, and well behaved to learn science best. I promise to

- Prepare for activities: I will listen to directions and make sure I understand them before I start
- Care for equipment: I will handle objects carefully and put them away when I am done
- Follow directions: I will do each step in order and I will not try unknown things
- Observe carefully: I will be as quiet and calm as possible so that I can learn more
- Keep careful records: I will write down my observations
- Clean up afterwards: I will wash my hands and my workspace
- Follow all safety rules

I will share good science safety with students and family so that I can be a good investigator.

(Signed) _____

               Student   Parent

There's the Bell

When planning science activities, make sure that you account for setup and cleanup time within the lesson. Distributing materials at the beginning of the class, collecting materials at the end, and cleaning up the work space and used equipment takes time to do properly. It's important that your students see this as part of their responsibility and that these tasks are an integral part of the entire science activity, so make sure that you schedule enough time for these housekeeping tasks.

If you have set a specific time to do a science activity, make sure that no one begins before everything is properly distributed and that everyone has stopped the activity when it is time to clean up. If students are doing their science activity in a center, make sure they know that cleaning up and preparing the center for the next student is very much a part of the activity. You may want to post a picture of the center's materials so students know what to leave there and in what condition. You won't have time to check every center just before dismissal.

Climbing the Walls

Every elementary teacher knows that a pleasant, informative classroom is one key to achievement. Many teachers are true artists when it comes to bulletin and trim boards and wall and ceiling enhancement. Even the students who "stare at the walls" learn in most classrooms.

You can put your talent for room enhancement to good use by keeping safety in mind. First, don't clutter. Paper is combustible. Mobiles and paper chains are fire hazards. Clutter makes kids trip and fall. Easily distracted students become more so in messy environments. And perhaps most importantly, clutter doesn't create a good impression of an orderly work—and learning—place.

Be rigorous about throwing things out. Don't fall into the pack-rat syndrome. You probably only need one good copy of that favorite lesson (on CD–ROM if possible). You can always get more coffee stirrers and straws—six won't help much anyway. (See Chapter 4 for storage tips.)

Use your board space to emphasize continuing themes and ongoing safety rules. Make a feature out of the classroom escape route and the eyewash station. Allow students to develop posters reminding one another of hand washing (Germs!) and proper disposal and recycling.

A Reputation for Excellence

Science is exciting, and for that reason the good science teacher can become something of a local hero in an elementary school. That's especially true if you create a science space: a classroom with mini-museums, displays, and interactive bulletin boards. But becoming the local gathering place has its own complications. The rules for safety must be so clear that even the casual visitor will learn them quickly.

One way to make sure that happens is to make your students all docents in your classroom. Give them a sense of ownership and encourage them to explain the rules—and why they are necessary—when someone comes in. You may want to set up a few test runs with some invited guests (the lunch mom or the custodian) so that you can test the students for both hospitality and safety consciousness.

Another easy way for students to share is via the computer. Very young students have enjoyed producing PowerPoint slides of their experiments, which can be scrolled in the media center or at parent night. Middle and elementary students have created great web pages for their school sites. Video clips of students pointing out safety hazards can be added to the web page. These are ways to share science without constant traffic in the room.

Remember, it is far better to have a reputation for inquiry than for chaos. If people who enter your room find they are challenged to think, you'll be the real local hero.

Setting High Expectations

As any veteran teacher knows, high achievement is the satisfying reward for setting high expectations for our students. This is as true for the use of safe procedures as for any other expectation. The more you make students responsible for using and enforcing safe laboratory and fieldwork procedures, the more easily safe practice becomes habit. Once you have established a classroom climate that is based on the expectation that students be as vigilant as you are in spotting safety hazards and eliminating them, you might find that fewer rules work better than rules for every step and procedure. The ultimate safety rule should be: Don't do anything that you know or think might be unsafe to yourself or to others.

With an inquiry-based science program, you are likely to encourage students to experiment, observe, and explore on their own, in addition to following your step-by-step instructions. However exploratory, the work must be done in a safe manner. There can be no experimentation with safety rules. When it comes to safety instructions and safe procedures, you need to be explicit and exacting. While safe practices support inquiry-based science, it is totally inappropriate to let students learn by trial and error when it comes to matters of safety. If you catch your students quoting you— you've succeeded.

SCI*LINKS*
THE WORLD'S A CLICK AWAY

Topic: safety in the classroom
Go to: *www.scilinks.org*
Code: SEL01

THE SAVVY SCIENCE TEACHER

Mr. Hernando's class is about to receive Lucia and Freya, a pair of gerbils, to care for and observe. In preparation for the animals' arrival, the class reads a trade book about gerbils in their natural habitat. When the cage and animals arrive, Mr. Hernando shows the children how to observe Lucia and Freya without disturbing them and how to clean and fill the water bottle hanging outside the cage. Immediately after the demonstration, Mr. Hernando goes to the sink and washes his hands, explaining why it is important to do. He also introduces a new center activity where students can use a variety of paper and markers to create illustrations of the new animals or hand washing posters to be hung next to the cage.

Connections

▶ American Chemical Society. 2001. *Safety in the Elementary (K–6) Science Classroom* (2nd ed.). Washington, D.C. American Chemical Society.
▶ NSTA Press. 1993. *Safety in the Elementary Classroom.* Arlington, Va.: NSTA Press.

Communities of Learners

Most of Michael J.'s assignments are done in cooperative groups. Students volunteer to be scribe, equipment clerk, technician, data analyst, and communicator. The labs were loud and disorganized at first, but now students move smoothly into investigations. You can never identify the special education or ESL students in each group because everyone is "sciencing."

Science for All

In science, goals of curiosity, logic, organization, and application rank high. When the reading and writing of informational text doesn't get in the way, we are often surprised at who does science best! Science is an ideal environment in which to use cooperative learning among students of varying abilities, building a true community of learners.

But day-to-day instruction seldom occurs in the ideal environment. When students with limited reading, mathematical, or communication skills work at laboratory activities, new challenges pose additional safety risks to everyone in the classroom. It's certainly possible—and good practice—to include students of almost any ability in a program that helps all learners achieve their personal best. But it will take some special precautions, extra organization, and the development of new sensitivities to make sure that learners of all abilities achieve their personal best in your classroom.

Least Restrictive Environments

Public Law 94–142, also known as the Individuals with Disabilities Education Act (IDEA), is a federal law passed in 1975 and reauthorized in 1990. It mandates that all children receive a free and appropriate public education, regardless of the level or severity of their disability. IDEA requires that, to the greatest extent possible, students with disabilities be educated with students who do not have disabilities. The law states that "unless a child's individualized education program requires some other arrangement, the child is (to be) educated in the school which he or she would attend if not disabled [Section 121a.522(c)]." It requires that removal of the child from the regular classroom occurs only when education in regular classes "with the use of supplementary aids and services cannot be achieved satisfactorily [Section 121a.550(2)]." That means that if it is possible and practical for a student to learn a subject in a regular education classroom, it must happen that way.

The Americans with Disabilities Act (ADA) of 1990 (*www.usdoj.gov/crt/ada/adahom1.htm*) prohibits discrimination against persons with disabilities. Like IDEA, this act mandates open access to regular educational facilities for persons who are disabled. But ADA goes beyond special education. Where IDEA would guide us in educating those students whose achievement is lower than their ability, ADA guides us in providing access to our facilities and programs by all members of the community—teachers, students, parents, and members of the general public. Complying with ADA is a general education function and falls to the regular education teacher.

Topic: learners with disabilities
Go to: *www.scilinks.org*
Code: SEL02

Every state has its own laws to implement IDEA and ADA; many of these regulations are more specific and detailed than the federal laws but all of them have the same philosophy and goals. Our communities of learners should be open to everyone.

It takes a special set of eyes and ears to make sure that our classrooms don't present barriers to any budding scientist. Many professional preparation programs ask prospective teachers to spend time in a wheelchair, on crutches, or with muffled vision or hearing. The view is certainly different from that perspective. The suggestions in this chapter won't cover every possible barrier but they can provide your school team with a place to start.

A Special Set of Eyes

Begin your observations by looking at the physical facilities in which you teach science. To accommodate a physically disabled student, you will need more space—probably twice as much—and specialized equipment. A wheelchair may be as wide as 86 cm and may take up even more room if the wheels are cambered (tilted out) for a paraplegic. Wall-mounted objects shouldn't be higher than 86 cm from the floor, and there should be at least 70 cm of knee space under the desks. To prevent pressure sores, many people with disabilities must sit on special cushions that increase knee space requirements. Sinks must not be more than 17 cm deep and must have "paddle" handles for students for whom turning the knobs would be a problem.

Your floor must be flat, even the path to the safety shower, and there should be no barriers such as taped-down wires or uneven carpet-tile interfaces. Make sure that there is a good exit path from the room in case of fire. Don't rely on a route through a fire door, which may close automatically if the fire alarm sounds. Glass-doored cabinets have many disadvantages but, most important, they are dangerous. They can shatter if a student pushes someone or throws something. They are also distracting.

Think about visually impaired students as you inspect your room. You may need labels in braille. Wall-mounted units should be placed above base cabinets. There should be no protruding edges or corners on casework and furnishings, an accommodation for visually impaired

- 86 cm aisles for wheelchairs
- 70 cm of knee space
- A sink no higher than 86 cm and no deeper than 17 cm with paddle handles
- Paddle handles on the exit door
- A clear exit with all flooring leveled or ramped, all entrances wider than 86 cm, and no access through automatic fire doors
- Clear sight lines from a sitting position
- Locked storage
- No protruding cabinets
- Access to the safety shower
- Braille labels on safety equipment
- Meyer Johnson symbols

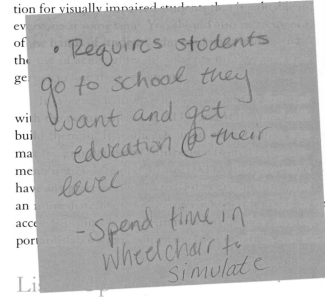

(handwritten note) • Requires students go to school they want and get education @ their level — Spend time in wheelchair to simulate

...ecial education student needs ...ou will probably need to add ...native sink stations.

At the elementary level, the most common disability is probably the least noticed—selected frequency hearing loss. Because the eustachian tubes of children are small and run horizontally, they are often filled with fluid. Allergies can also cause fluid-filled ears. This causes hearing loss that can be slight or very severe. During the cold and flu season, as many as half of the kindergarteners in any given group may have some degree of hearing impairment due to fluid buildup.

The most frustrating part of the hearing-loss problem is that it can occur at only certain frequencies; for example, students may be unable to discriminate fricatives such as /s/, /f/, or /sh/. In very young children, where the development of phonemic awareness is a crucial part of learning to read, even a slight distortion of sound can be a major problem. The problem is exacerbated by the way we used to construct classrooms. We like space and, in developmental rooms, we like to minimize noise. So we create high ceilings and carpeted floors—sound absorbers that prevent students from hearing well. Any wonder that May or Kim doesn't pay attention to our directions in science? Many schools have countered the problem of hearing with sound-amplification systems. These systems involve a small (lavalier) microphone on the teacher's lapel and speakers in the ceiling or walls. The amplification is not great but enough to clarify what you say.

These systems have an important safety value for you as a teacher, too. Many years of extended abuse of the vocal cords (that "teacher voice" we develop) can gradually erode the tissues. Since there is no pain sensation in the vocal cords, the damage can occur without any clear signs. The teacher will feel tired, the voice will crack, and colds will have a tendency to settle in the compromised tissues. Two kinds of damage can occur: polyps, which must be removed surgically, and erosion of the vocal cord tissue (*myast...*) ..., you have the right to reasonable a...

Accom...

Being able t... learning science but it often is. Co... s:

- Many o... form, and the way you assess u...

- When a... ploration may be only availabl...

- Learnin... ential procedures if the sequenc... -disabled students and student... equential procedures.

- Meyer ... dition to written and verbal instructions.

[Handwritten note overlaid on page:] —Safety Directions in written form * (more visuals) * Always State orally

Begin by giving every direction orally and be conscious of the reading level of your activity sheets. Put major directions on a chart board or an overhead transparency and have them displayed during the activity. Before a group begins its work, have the students repeat their safety directions to one another. Consider performance assessments for basic safety skills such as using droppers, wearing eye protection, and using tools. Be sure to keep written records to track and ensure that every student has received safety instructions and has been assessed for safety skills.

Atoms Aren't the Only Things that Jiggle

Heterogeneous classes almost always include students with behavioral challenges as well as those with physical and learning disabilities. ADHD (attention deficit hyperactivity disorder) is becoming more common among students today. Drug and alcohol exposure during prenatal development, allergies, or stress may decrease students' ability to make appropriate judgments.

Even students who have no systemic handicaps can have low attention spans. Your students spend far more time in front of frenetically paced media than they spend in your classroom. There is no way that a science lab could be safe at the pace of MTV!

In order to minimize accidents and increase students' attention span, begin with small steps. Start with five-minute experiences. Encourage careful observation. Have students rank one another's work. Ask that directions be repeated one or more times. Never plan a classroom activity for many more minutes than the students' age in years.

Keep your classroom neat and organized, giving students some of that responsibility. Maintain a lot of extra space so that a sudden move can't result in an overturned piece of furniture. That may mean giving away a little of your furniture or boxing up some of your treasures that you have kept "just in case you need them." Make sure that your grading system rewards responsible self-control.

Students with autism are usually very good at following directions and instructions and often are very visually oriented. Science activities can reward their abilities to produce graphic rather than verbal representations of their work and understanding. Many teachers have found science to be a magic key to better attention and better performance in behaviorally challenged students. With these tips, you may too.

Tips for Better Control of ADHD Students

- Keep every experience short, including labs.
- Post directions and have students act out the essential safety precautions.
- Carefully plan the composition of student groups.
- Don't keep a cluttered room. Put away everything unnecessary.
- Keep the room as quiet as possible. Discourage loud voices (but of course, allow talking).
- Have a plan to get students' attention that doesn't involve shouting; try a special clap, a blinking light, or a sign. Practice it in advance.
- Consider assistive technologies like word processors for notes.
- Give small leadership responsibilities to reward good behavior.

To Your Good Health

The tips on the previous page help teachers deal with students with long-term or permanent disabilities. But teachers must also accommodate and take steps to minimize temporary disabilities and illnesses in the science classroom.

The most common temporary disabilities in classrooms are colds. Despite the virus's status as "common," the problems caused by colds are becoming more complex. Now that there isn't an "at-home" parent in most homes, there is a far greater tendency for students to be sent to school sick. Teachers need tricks to cope.

Allergies may look like colds but they persist and aren't infectious. The same rules for coughs and colds should apply because infections take advantage of inflamed tissues. Be aware of the possible presence of allergens in your room. (See Chapter 5). Always remember that allergic reactions can become life-threatening conditions very quickly. If a student develops hives that are larger than a dime or are spreading, or if the student has any sign of respiratory distress, call for medical help immediately.

Do not provide medication—prescription or over-the-counter—to any student. Even the most common over-the-counter medication can cause a reaction. Never administer medicine of any kind. You are not qualified, authorized, or insured to do so. And don't encourage students to bring their own medications on the bus or keep them in their lockers. If a student needs medicine at school, it should be in its own (prescription) bottle with directions provided by the physician. It should be administered in the office in the presence of a trained professional. Check your state and district policies, which may state the number of adult witnesses needed and types of medication that schools can dispense.

Fighting Infection in the Classroom

▶ Start reminding parents in your newsletters early: "Please keep sick children at home."

▶ Keep tissues handy and reinforce their use.

▶ Have soap and warm water near the sink; students and teachers should wash their hands.

▶ Ask that your room be kept relatively cool.

▶ If students come to school very ill, send them home.

▶ Keep non-latex rubber gloves handy.

There are many other communicable diseases for which a teacher should be alert. Scabies (a bacterial skin infection) and head lice are highly contagious in the school environment. Students should be immunized against measles and chicken pox, but teachers should still be familiar with the appearance of those rashes.

Learn the appearance of poison ivy/oak rashes and insect bites as well. The appearance of any rashes should be referred to the school nurse or other designated school health professional.

A SIDEBAR ON SIDE EFFECTS

Because of advertisements in the media, students are often very casual about drugs. Both prescription and over-the-counter medications are heavily advertised, and characters on television use drugs casually. A student investigation of the side effects of common drugs is a valuable research project; this can be done through the Internet.

One drug that merits special discussion is Ritalin. Many students take Ritalin each day, often in a location that is quite visible to other students. There have been increasing incidents of Ritalin abuse and sale of pills on school campuses. A report on the purposes of Ritalin and the side effects, especially for those who are not diagnosed with ADHD, would help all of your students become safer citizens.

A Little Help from Your Friends

Many schools are encouraging the use of co-teachers or aides in order to integrate special needs students into the regular education classroom. This can be a tremendous help and a valued safety measure. But the teacher(s) must take a great deal of responsibility to make the partnership work effectively.

Co-teachers may not have the preparation in teaching science that the regular education teacher has. But they will have special skills in assessment, behavior modification, and remedial reading that can help special needs students succeed in science. Treat the co-teacher as a partner. Plan jointly and alternate the role of lead teacher. It takes extended, in-depth conversation for a co-teaching relationship to work well.

Paraprofessionals also require an allocation of planning time. You should always remember that you are the responsible professional and the science expert. Don't expect your paraprofessional to learn along with the students. Go over the safety precautions—including all of the things that might happen—in advance and insist that paras be given paid time to learn the science methods they need.

Treasuring Diversity

There is great value in a heterogeneous classroom. The sensitivity that students develop when they work in groups with students of differing abilities can't be overestimated. Encourage your students to appreciate that in a community of learners, science is a social endeavor. And encourage them to understand that they are responsible, not only for their own safety, but for the safety of others in their group and in their classroom. They'll be better scientists for it.

THE SAVVY SCIENCE TEACHER

Michael J.'s students love technology and love to teach one another. He encourages them to prepare PowerPoint presentations for the class. To do that, each student gets to use an electronic camera and prepare one slide. The entire group's slides are merged (using the "Insert" tool) into one presentation that the class views. The class grades each group's show using a rubric they all understand.

For their safety lesson, each student in a group demonstrates one safety technique: wearing eye protection, cutting safely, putting equipment away, using the proper equipment, wearing safe clothing, and following directions. Students prepare a safety tip of their own, and their text is typed under their pictures. A cycling presentation plays during Parent Night and earns the "Academy Award" for Mike's students.

Connections

▶ American Association for the Advancement of Science (AAAS). 1991. *Barrier Free in Brief: Laboratories and Classrooms in Science and Engineering.* Washington, D.C.: American Association for the Advancement of Science.

▶ Reese, Kenneth M. 1985. *Teaching Chemistry to Physically Handicapped Students.* Washington, D.C. American Chemical Society.

Where Science Happens

It is said that the walls brought ancient Jericho down—and the walls were certainly defeating Juan's science program. They were too close, too thin, and too cluttered. Of course, the leaking ceiling and the wobbly cabinets didn't help either. It sometimes seemed that Juan's best ideas were buried under a stack of maintenance requests.

A State of Mind and Body

It's often said that science is a way of knowing—a state of mind. But science also requires a safe and secure environment for active young bodies. The condition of school facilities is an important component of a safe and successful program.

Government studies have indicated that more than 40 percent of school buildings are in such poor condition that they are unsafe for children. Even new facilities can be too crowded or architecturally unsuited for exploration. It's important to recognize the recommended facilities standards for school science, whether or not those ideal conditions can be achieved right away. You can still set goals and modify your program as you work toward them.

While many elementary schools include a designated science space—a lab or discovery room that can be scheduled by teachers for special investigations—it is also important to integrate science into all subjects, all the time, and to use "teachable moments." So most educators recommend that all classrooms be built with the basic requirements for hands-on science. For elementary rooms that includes hot and cold running water, safety eyewash, lockable storage, flat desk surfaces, fire protection, protected electrical supply, and project/display areas.

To support science, the ideal elementary room should have

- A minimum of 4 m² per student (96 m² for a class of 24)
- Additional space to accommodate students with disabilities
- 1.4 m² for each desktop computer station
- 0.9 m² per student of preparation space for the teacher
- 22 m² of lockable storage area for a class of 24
- A ceiling height of 3 m
- Two escape routes (a second door or large window without screen)
- Ventilation of at least four air changes per hour
- Hot and cold running water with soap
- Eyewash facilities
- Fire protection

Source: Biehle, J., L. Motz, and S. West. 1999. *NSTA Guide to School Science Facilities.* Arlington, Va.: National Science Teachers Association.

Eyewashes

We recommend plumbed systems with fresh running water for eyewashes. Bottled eyewashes are not recommended. There is a protist that lives in water that can cause "river blindness"; it's been found in classroom eyewashes that are never flushed.

Safety = Space

Your classroom space is an important safety factor. Class size is the most reliable indicator of safety in science. The data are clear: Crowded children have more accidents. Minimum space requirements are listed in the box on the right. Where they can't be met, limit enrollment! Document the labs and program elements that you can't do safely in today's space to help plan for tomorrow's renovations or new construction.

Take a few minutes to look around. Can you supervise every place where students can be? If not, consider rearranging your furniture and adding strategically placed parabolic mirrors. Can students get to the sink or eyewash quickly? If not, give away some of the furniture.

Even the most spacious classrooms can be cluttered by excess furniture. Teachers tend to be pack rats, saving stuff *just in case*. These collections become safety hazards and reduce your working space. Keep no more than one steel filing cabinet of old papers and plans. Scan your favorite exercises onto a CD-ROM and get rid of the paper. Don't block escape routes with furniture.

Come in early one morning and conduct an imaginary emergency drill: What if an accidental spill occurred here? Where would the students run? Could they all, even a disabled student, get out quickly? (Remember, some fire doors close automatically.) Could they get to the sink? Is there room to "stop, drop, and roll?"

You Have to Break Some Eggs

Many teachers face renovation projects during the school year. Having workers on site creates special challenges to your program and your students' safety. It is important to take renovations into consideration as you plan the program and to communicate your program needs to the on-site supervisors.

Your school's renovation project should have a familiar manager close by to ensure safety in construction. That means effective barriers and unobstructed escape routes. If the on-site supervisor misses something, call quickly.

Use the construction and the construction personnel to help teach safety. Give students a tour around the limits of the work and explain where they may not go. Warn them to report any stray tools, nails, or other products.

Be conscious of ventilation patterns that might be disrupted during construction. If your room is temporarily tighter, or if you have less natural light than usual, modify your program accordingly.

Take advantage of the workers' expertise if possible. Invite an electrician to explain how to handle plugs safely. Ask a painter to explain fumes and chemical safety.

Behind the Labels

You are responsible for *every* material you bring into or accept in your classroom. You must know what it is, what it can do, and how it should be stored. You are also responsible for ensuring that others in the building, such as the custodian and principal, know the information ahead of time in case of an emergency.

The federal government requires that manufacturers supply Materials Safety Data Sheets (MSDS) for everything they produce. These are documents in a standard format that can be obtained for every material in your room—including markers, crayons, cleaning supplies, glues, and paints. The MSDSs should be available in the office and duplicate copies should be in your classroom. Your central office and local fire department should also maintain a list of all potentially hazardous materials to properly respond to emergencies. For more information on MSDSs, see Chapter 4.

Teach children to respect chemicals. Discuss potential hazards. Teachers have been held liable for serious accidents when students stole chemicals from unlocked cabinets and used them to make explosions at home. (See Chapter 4 for true stories.) Don't allow children to handle concentrated chemicals in your room, and limit cleaning to dish soap and vinegar. These lessons can help prevent accidental poisoning and instill respect for chemicals in their world.

SCI*LINKS.*
THE WORLD'S A CLICK AWAY

Topic: chemical safety
Go to: *www.scilinks.org*
Code: SEL03

The Eyes Have It

Remember the days when renovators were covering up school windows to save heat? Now researchers tell us there is strong evidence that student achievement is higher in natural light. We also know that some fluorescent lights exacerbate hyperactivity and headaches, and make computer screens more difficult to read.

Lighting is also an important safety factor. Make sure your storage areas, deep cabinets, and corners are lighted. Also investigate whether your escape routes would be visible if the power suddenly went out. Some schools have emergency backup lighting for this purpose.

MR. B, CHANNEL 6 IS ON THE LINE

Bay Elementary thought its long construction project was at an end until one Monday morning when a strange odor wafted down the halls. No one could identify it but everyone knew it was unpleasant.

Rumors spread like wildfire. It was toxic—it was corrosive. Teachers and children began to cover their faces, and soon several sensitive students were gasping. A visiting parent called a local news channel, another called 911. Soon reporters, police, and ambulances were hovering, and the whole school had to be evacuated. A dozen students were treated for possible respiratory distress.

Meanwhile, the principal was investigating. Workers had been in the building on Saturday applying a coat of sealer on concrete under an overhead fan. What was the chemical? No one knew. No Material Safety Data Sheet (MSDS) was available. Hours later the errant workers were tracked down, the chemical identified, and its very low toxicity documented. It was a harmless—but rather odorous—varnish and only a very small quantity had been applied. Because the weekend had been rainy it hadn't dried, and its location under a fan had made the odor spread. A single MSDS on the principal's desk would have prevented a countywide emergency and a major public relations fiasco.

Fire Protection

Schools are built with fire prevention as part of the basic design. But even the best design can be defeated by thoughtless use. It is important that teachers understand the protections our buildings provide and support them with good practices.

Open flames are seldom needed in an elementary classroom. If you need a flame, use a candle that is wider than it is tall. Never use alcohol burners or gas at the elementary level.

Your classroom was probably designed to have two secure exits for fire control. One may be a large window without a screen. Have you screened that window? Have you blocked a fire exit with furniture?

The wall coverings and ceilings of your classroom are fire resistant. Have you covered them with paper or hung combustible materials from the walls or ceilings? Make sure your holiday decorations and displays follow district policy and fire codes.

You need an ABC fire extinguisher that is checked regularly. (Check the date on the tag and notify your building administrator if the inspection date tag is missing or the inspection is not up to date.) Learn when and how to use the fire extinguisher (your local fire department may be a good resource) and show every student where it is located. Your school should also have a smoke detector and an identifiable fire alarm. Make sure your students know what visual and audio signals are used to indicate a fire emergency and how to respond immediately to those signals. Post the fire escape route and practice regularly. Make sure students understand the difference between a fire drill and the procedures for windstorms or earthquakes. While you probably won't need a safety shower for elementary labs, have a blanket and practice stop, drop, and roll in case of emergencies.

At the elementary level, local fire departments may be eager to send firefighters to your class to present fire-safety instruction. If this service is available to you, preview the program and use it if it's appropriate. Your local fire personnel may also do a courtesy inspection to advise you of ways you can make your facilities safer.

A Partnership with Your Student Scientists

Scientists use specialized equipment to do their investigations. Your students will respect their science experiences more if they are partners in the inventory, storage, and safe keeping of that equipment in your classroom.

Experts recommend a separate, lockable preparation space for every teacher from the earliest grades onward. It should have good air supply and direct outdoor ventilation. If this isn't possible in your school, invest in vented, locked cabinets for all of your chemicals. Shelves should have lips to prevent spills. Corners should not be sharp because students might bump into them. Glass doors are not recommended for cabinets. They look attractive when they are empty but get cluttered and tempt students. They can break if a student throws something or a tussle occurs.

Store chemicals by category, not alphabetically. (See Chapter 4.) Date your acquisitions and dispose of old stock appropriately. Keep only what you need, and don't

A Basic Science Equipment List for Elementary Classes

▶ Aquaria, terraria, cages
▶ Microscopes, compound and stereoscopic
▶ Hand lenses
▶ Balances and spring scales
▶ Maps and globes
▶ Weather instruments
▶ Grow lights and planters
▶ Physics dynamics carts
▶ Temperature and motion interfaces (calculator or computer)
▶ Calculators and meter sticks
▶ Timers and stopwatches
▶ Digital camera and computer(s)
▶ Plastic and borosilicate glassware
▶ Eye protection and sterilizing facilities
▶ Collection boxes and nets
▶ Batteries, bulbs, wires, and electrical equipment
▶ Motion detectors

See Chapter 6 for a basic chemical inventory.

accept hand-me-downs or donations from the high school, parents, or industry; they will probably be stronger and far more dangerous than you need.

Prepare chemicals for labs before the students arrive. Remove only a small quantity of the chemicals you will be using and keep the stock bottles locked up during class. A suggested elementary inventory is listed in Chapter 6.

Power Up

When teachers are asked to rate their classrooms, space is often their first complaint. But power ranks a close second. As we add more electronic devices to our programs, there never seem to be enough electrical receptacles in the right places for today's classrooms.

Your classroom should have at least four separate circuits, each protected by a ground fault interrupter (GFI) device that shuts off the circuit in case of shock. If you are tripping circuit breakers, you don't have enough power. This happens most often with devices that generate heat, like hot plates and electric heaters. Remember, you can't just add plugs—your school must add circuits to solve your power problem. Don't use those "socket multipliers" that are sold in hardware stores because they are dangerous and can damage equipment.

Extension cords pose both fire and tripping hazards. Never allow loose cords to cross student aisles and pathways. If your school installs floor sockets, make sure they do not project above the floor to stub toes or trip students. If you occasionally need a plug in the center of a room for a rare occasion, cover the cord with heavy tape and remove quickly after use.

A Room for All Activities—Science Included

A well-designed, self-contained elementary classroom should allow you to teach science both by using centers and by integrating science fully with other classroom activities. If you have the opportunity to furnish a room, be creative! Consider flexibility and safety together—they are very compatible goals. Make sure there is enough space and ventilation, adequate exits, and hot water. Request natural lighting and extra parabolic (nonreflective) lights for close work. Include a drinking fountain that can be used as an eyewash and a sink with a wet (tiled) area for cleanup.

Furnish the integrated classroom with flat desks that can be grouped for cooperative investigations or large tables. Avoid stools. Move the chairs away and let the students stand for hands-on activities; it's much safer in case of a spill. Consider displaying the list of basic equipment (previous page), with word or picture signs identifying where each item is stored.

Special equipment and other aids needed to ensure a safe environment for special needs students should be identified in Individual Education Plans (IEPs). These plans should be carefully reviewed in planning for the physical space as well as for instructional strategies.

Signs and Symbols

Marking your classroom can make it both educational and safe. First, make sure your classroom number is clearly identified and that your students know what it is in case of emergency. Post important phone numbers and extensions in your room right beside the fire, storm, and earthquake procedures. Practice identifying standard pictograms.

| Poison | Combustible | Biohazard |
| Explosive | High Voltage | Corrosive |

Then make classroom signage part of your class's organization. Label where things go and where they don't go. Use lots of pictures and symbols as well as worded labels and instructions. Keep charts for maintenance and organism-care responsibilities. Let your students know where your fire protection equipment is and when it is maintained. Keep eye protection on display with appropriate signs for use and cleaning.

Clear markings contribute to clear thinking. They also convey the idea that safety is a shared responsibility for all science investigators.

If the Walls Won't Come Down

Facilities are the least flexible part of a school program. While there may be long-term remodeling goals for most buildings, many teachers find that their current situation is very limited. What do you do if you know that your classroom doesn't meet safety and facility standards and there is no immediate relief in sight?

First, clean up and clean out. Make space by removing everything from the room that isn't needed. You may need to box up materials by month or season. Then take a hard look at your furnishings. Can you invest in more flexible pieces or trade with another teacher? Can you rearrange to create more space?

Prioritize your maintenance requests and *document them.* Don't fall victim to the "they won't do it anyway" attitude. Repeat your requests at regular intervals and explain to your administrator what choices you are forced to make until you can get repairs made.

Downsize your lab experiences and your storage needs. Then remember that science is *everywhere.* Take your students outside to study not just biology but also physics. Take them to the grocery store to study chemistry. Be creative while you are being safe.

Connections

- Biehle, J., L. Motz, and S. West. 1999. *NSTA Guide to Science Facilities.* Arlington, Va.: NSTA Press.
- Lowery, L., ed. 2000. Appendix C in *NSTA Pathways to the Science Standards—Elementary School Edition.* Arlington, VA.: National Science Teachers Association.

The Science Place

Making every classroom "science-able" allows an elementary teacher to take advantage of every teachable moment. It's important to work with your administrator so that he or she knows not just what you want but why those requirements are important. So along with good facilities, make communication a goal.

THE SAVVY SCIENCE TEACHER

As an August graduate, Phil was thrilled to have a job. A local third grade teacher decided at the last minute to take early retirement and cruise the world. But when Phil entered the room in which he would teach in just 48 hours, panic set in. It looked like the souvenirs from that cruise had been gathered 20 years in advance! The room was so crowded with furniture, books, and supplies he could hardly navigate between the desks.

Phil put on his game face and grabbed a rolling barrel. He also borrowed a flatbed scanner from the media center. With the help of some early-arriving students, he scanned one of each set of sample lessons to disk and recycled the rest. He donated a large rocking chair to the media center and two sets of old literature series books to the P.T.A. An unlabeled bone collection found its way to the barrel. He negotiated a trade of six large tables for smaller ones from the art teacher down the hall.

Phil found one cabinet filled with cleaning supplies and science reagents. He called an 800 number and found that he was able to run some of the materials down the sink. He donated two bottles of stronger chemicals to the high school and relabeled the remaining six bottles with date and condition. While the cabinet keys were long lost, he was able to purchase child safety locks for one set of cabinets in which his now tiny chemical stores could be safely kept.

One day to go. Phil rearranged his furniture to clear a path to the emergency exit window. A small but complete set of lab glassware was found in a variety of hiding places around the room. Phil washed it and stored it under an inventory sign. He washed the aquarium too and began his life science collection with a few donated guppies and two blooming plants. Then it was time to recharge. The real "life" in the classroom was on its way—22 eager third graders ready to explore. With more space and organization, they were bound to find success.

Finders Keepers

> *Geri G. is a frequent shopper at garage sales. At various sites in her neighborhood she's found a rocking chair, two file cabinets, three bookshelves, and plastic milk crates for her classroom. Yet she never has enough room—and increasingly, she can't find what she's looking for. Often she finds it easier to recreate an activity sheet than locate it. Yet when Geri's principal told her to clean up and clean out, she was torn: "How can I live without this stuff?"*

4

Storage Secrets

It takes a lot of "stuff" to conduct an activity-based science program. Teachers often use personal funds to purchase materials to use in their classes. They also save a lot from year to year and collect items for possible future use. But saving things also requires a lot of storage space that may not be available. So a balance must be struck because clutter presents a safety problem in classrooms, particularly classrooms with active science programs. Being able to distinguish between those truly useful items to keep from year to year, finding spaces and ways to store items neatly and safely, and knowing how to properly dispose of unneeded items are important skills to learn and practice regularly.

Build Safety in from the Start

If a new building or classroom is contemplated, be sure that storage is given appropriate consideration. There should be storage that is easily accessible by children with little or no adult assistance. There should also be storage that is completely inaccessible to children, lockable, and preferably in a separate storage/preparation room. Experts recommend three cubic meters or more of storage space for each student in the class.

In a typical classroom, storage should be well distributed throughout the room, occupying space on at least three of the four walls. For elementary classrooms, good storage can also be in the form of movable units that also serve as space dividers. If you are using movable units, be certain that there are means to lock the wheels and keep them solidly in place. Most state and local building codes also specify that non-

Storing Chemicals Safely

- Locks and lips—good cabinets have both.
- Store chemicals by category, not alphabetically.
- Don't store flammable chemicals in the classroom, and never store them with combustible materials.
- Don't keep strong corrosives (e.g., acids and bases) in an elementary classroom at all. Store weak acids and bases, such as soaps and vinegar, separate from flammables.
- Keep a notebook of MSDSs.
- Write the telephone number of your nearest Poison Control Center in front of your lesson plan book and/or telephone book, and post it near your telephone.

movable cabinets must be anchored to the wall so they cannot possibly cause injury in a tipping accident. Even if there is no such code in your district, check all your cabinet and storage units for proper stability and insist on anchoring the units. Also include some flat storage drawers that can accommodate posters and students' easel work. Avoid having glass doors on cabinets. They are breakable and tempting and almost always look messy. Prevent spills by having lips on the edges of cabinet shelves.

Cabinets where chemicals are stored should always be lockable, and students should never have the keys. Build security into your routine. Take a little out, put the stock bottle away, and lock it up. Store chemicals well back, and don't leave chemical cabinets open during class activities.

There are special cabinets sold for corrosive chemicals such as acids and bases. They are made of special plastics that will not dissolve or corrode as metals do. If your program requires acids, you need a special cabinet for them. In most cases you should be able to find suitable substitute activities that do not require you to use or store strong corrosives (See Chapter 6 for safer alternatives.)

Flammable chemicals also require a specialized vented cabinet made of metal. If you don't have a fireproof storage space, keep a flammable chemical (such as rubbing alcohol) in a flameproof section of custodial storage.

Remember, you can tell the hazards of a chemical by the special symbol on the side. (See Chapter 3, **Signs and Symbols.**)

THREE TRUE STORYGE STORIES

▸ An elementary school teacher accepted a sample of potassium from the secondary school and kept it in the storeroom with a collection of elements. It was stolen and carried home in a student's pocket. The student's body heat caused it to ignite, causing severe burns.

▸ A middle school teacher reported to police that she thought some chemicals were missing but could not be sure because the inventory was old. Intense investigation revealed that a student had been gradually removing the chemicals to his bedroom in the hope of making explosives.

▸ A teacher moved into a new classroom in a renovated middle school where she found several rusty containers of chemicals, including one with the illegible notation: "P...Acid." Fearing that the container held picric acid, the school had to call the bomb squad to remove the old bottle.

4

Age Discrimination

Chemicals are not like fine wines. They do not grow better as they age. In fact, many can become very dangerous. Consider just a few examples:

▸ Ethers can break down to explosive components as they get older. Just turning the cap can cause an explosion.

▸ Picric acid, which once was used to preserve specimens but should never be in a school, becomes an unstable explosive when dried out.

▸ Many powdered reagents become so hard that they cannot be removed from their stock bottles.

Date every purchase. Buy only what you need for one year, even if it's cheaper to buy in quantity. Consider the costs and hazards of disposal before you purchase, and get rid of all old chemicals properly at the end of the year.

When You Absolutely Have to Have It

An MSDS is a standard document that is available for every chemical manufactured and/or sold in the United States. It contains specific information in a specific format so that a teacher, chemist, doctor, or emergency medical technician can find what they need immediately. Many teachers don't realize that they are available for such common items as glue, paste, soap, and markers as well as exotic chemicals.

Topic: chemical safety
Go to: *www.scilinks.org*
Code: SEL03

Federal and many state laws require that MSDSs be available **all the time** for **every chemical** you use or store in your classroom. They must be accessible to the administrative and noninstructional staff, the teacher and students, and to emergency personnel who might enter the building. That normally means that there will be at least two complete sets of documents, one in the classroom and one in the office. Your local fire department should also be provided with an inventory and a map showing the specific location of the MSDSs.

Elementary teachers are often surprised to learn that "every chemical" includes common, everyday items such as crayons, markers, dish and hand soaps, and food materials such as baking soda that they bring into their classrooms.

When chemicals are ordered through normal school supply vendors, your requisition should specify that the vendor "Provide MSDS with order." Your school office personnel should know where to look for the MSDS and where to file it, since the orders may come in during the summer. They should also know to refuse a shipment that lacks an MSDS.

If you need to bring chemicals from home or purchase them at a convenience store because they are less expensive, you must get the MSDS yourself. You can sometimes find a telephone number on the bottle. A good source of MSDS information for common household products is the Vermont Safety Information Resources Inc. site (*www.siri.org*). (See **Connections** at the end of this chapter.)

MATERIAL SAFETY DATA SHEET—BLEACH LAUNDRY ORGANIC CHLORINE
(Abbreviated version)

General Information

Item Name: BLEACH LAUNDRY ORGANIC CHLORINE
Company's Name and Address: _____
Company's Emerg Ph #: _____

Ingredients/Identity Information

Proprietary: NO Signs/Symptoms Of Overexp: INHALATION: IRRITATION TO NOSE, THROAT, MOUTH SEVERE IRRITATION AND/OR BURNS. EYES: SEVERE IRRITATION AND/OR BURNS CAN OCCUR.
Emergency/First Aid Proc: EYES: FLUSH W/LG AMTS WATER—15 MIN,

---

OCCASIONALLY LIFT UPPER/LOWER LIDS. CALL DOCTOR. SKIN: FLUSH—15 MIN. CALL DOCTOR. REMOVE CONTAM CLOTHING AND WASH BEFORE REUSE. INGEST: DON'T INDUCE VOMIT. DRINK LG AMTS WATER. DON'T GIVE ANYTHING BY MOUTH IF PERSON IS UNCONSCIOUS OR HAVING CONVULSIONS. INHALE: REMOVE TO FRESH AIR. IF BREATH HARD, GIVE OXY. KEEP WARM/REST. IF BREATH STOPS, GIVE CPR. CALL DOCTOR.

Precautions for Safe Handling and Use

Steps If Matl Released/Spill: IF SPILL IS DRY, CLEAN UP W/CLEAN, DRY DEDICATED EQUIP & PLACE IN CLEAN, DRY CNTNR. SPILL RESIDUES: DISPOSE OF AS NOTED BELOW. NEUTRALIZE MAT'L FOR DISPOSAL. CALL 1-800-654-6911
Waste Disposal Method: PRODUCT DOES NOT MEET CRITERIA OF HAZARDOUS WASTE.

CARE TO PREVENT CONTAMINATION FROM THE USE OF THIS PRODUCT. COOL, DRY, WELL-VENT AREA. DO NOT STORE ABOVE 140 F OR IN PAPER/CARDBOARD. KEEP CLOSED & FROM MOISTURE.
Other Precautions: ADDITIONAL RESPIRATORY PROTECTION NECESSARY WHEN SMALL, DAMP SPILLS INVOLVING PRODUCT OCCUR, WHICH RELEASES CHLORINE GAS. FULL FACE CARTRIDGE-TYPE NIOSH APPROVED RESPIRATORY W/CHLORINE CARTRIDGE RECOMMENDED. USE SELF-CNTND BREATHING APPAR.Ingredient: SODIUM CHLORIDE
Ingredient Sequence Number: 01
Percent: 45-50

Proprietary: NO
Ingredient: SODIUM TRIPOLYPHOSPHATE
Ingredient Sequence Number: 02
Percent: 25-30

Proprietary: NO
Ingredient: SODIUM DICHLORO-S-TRIAZINETRIONE
Ingredient Sequence Number: 03
Percent: 24-28

Fire and Explosion Hazard Data

Extinguishing Media: USE MEDIA TO CONTROL A SURROUNDING FIRE. DO NOT USE DRY CHEMICAL EXTINGUISHERS CONTAINING AMMONIUM COMPOUNDS.
Special Fire Fighting Proc: USE WATER TO COOL CONTAINERS EXPOSED TO FIRE. SMALL FIRES—USE WATER SPRAY OR FOG. LARGE FIRES—USE HEAVY DELUGE OR FOG STREAMS.
Unusual Fire And Expl Hazrds: NONE. REQUIRED BEFORE EXTINGUISHMENT CAN BE ACCOMPLISHED. THE USE OF SELF-CONTAINED BREATHING APPARATUS IS REQUIRED IN A FIRE WHERE THIS PRODUCT IS INVOLVED.

Reactivity Data

Stability: YES
Cond To Avoid (Stability): ELEVATED TEMPERATURES (ABOVE 140 F)
Materials To Avoid: OTHER OXIDIZERS, NITROGEN CONTAINING COMPOUNDS, DRY FIRE EXTINGUISHERS CONTAINING MONO-AMMONIUM PHOSPHATE.
Hazardous Decomp Products: NITROGEN TRICHLORIDE, CHLORINE, CARBON MONOXIDE.

Health Hazard Data

Route Of Entry—Inhalation: YES
Route Of Entry—Skin: YES
Route Of Entry—Ingestion: YES
Health Haz Acute And Chronic: INHALATION OF HIGH CONCENTRATIONS CAN RESULT IN PERMANENT LUNG DAMAGE. CHRONIC INHALATION CAN ALSO CAUSE PERMANENT LUNG DAMAGE. SKIN: PROLONGED EXPOSURE MAY CAUSE DESTRUCTION OF THE DERMIS WITH IMPAIRMENT OF SIGHT TO PROPERLY REGENERATE. EYES: MAY CAUSE VISION IMPAIRMENT AND CORNEAL DAMAGE.

But I Might Need It Some Day

Almost every teacher has experienced the problem—this year's budget is small, next year's may be nonexistent. You bought these washers and soda straws yourself. If you don't put them in the drawer, you may need to buy more next year. So the drawer fills up with three washers, four soda straws, two big alligator clips, a couple of dying batteries, and some spilled fish food.

Rule 1: Anything you haven't used in two years you probably don't need. Or, more realistically, when you decide you need it you probably won't be able to find it and will buy another one.

Rule 2: Never accept hand-me-downs from the high school, generous parents, or industry (except perhaps for hand lenses or rock samples). Reagent chemicals are far stronger than you need. Chemicals have shelf lives and your hand-me-downs may be of uncertain age. The bottles may have been contaminated by use. As the new owner, you will become responsible for disposal, which may be very costly.

Rule 3: Date your purchases. (See **Age Discrimination** in this chapter.) If you have access to a chemical database software program, enter each purchase. At the very least, mark the date of purchase with indelible marker on the container.

Rule 4: Get a good storage guide for everything you buy. (The Flinn Scientific Catalog is a very good free source of safe storage and handling information.)

Rule 5: If you can reduce the size of your supplies, do so. Scan worksheets to disk. Keep a web address list rather than catalogs for supplies. Almost all companies have online catalogs now.

Rule 6: Never ignore a spill or a cloudy film on the inside of a chemical-storage cabinet. They are indicators that the chemicals you have stored are reacting or decomposing. Never leave a jar with a rusted cap or crack in the cabinet. Spills and vapors are dangerous in themselves and even more so when they get together.

Student Storage

Student storage has become a major safety issue in schools because of the increased incidence of student violence. Many schools are moving away from hallway lockers because they are not easily searched and require trips outside the teacher's supervisory view. The elementary alternative is "cubbies" in the classrooms, but they should be monitored to ensure that they are neat, clean, and not overflowing.

Book bags and coats should remain in cubbies or closets, not shoved under desks. In an emergency, items on the floor could block exit or access to the eyewash. Items slung over the back of a chair can make it unstable and more likely to tip over. Make sure the cubbies get emptied every night so that things don't pile up.

It's Yours for Life

Did you know that from the moment you purchase a chemical you are responsible for its disposal? Even if you turn it over to someone else, the fact is that if they dispose of it improperly, the chain of responsibility can bring the liability back to you.

Imagine that you bought the heavy metal salt ammonium dichromate many years ago. (It was once recommended for model volcanoes.) You have a large jar of it left. In a moment of weakness, you throw it in the trash. A student steals it from the dumpster and takes it home. Bored with it, he dumps it in the garden where a cat gets into it and dies. You could be held responsible for the death of the cat. The chain of responsibility goes even farther. If your jar had made it to the local landfill, and if a water source was contaminated a decade later, you could be found negligent.

Disposal is complex and can be very expensive. It can cost ten times more to dispose of an item than to purchase it. Look up the disposal issues before you purchase something. If it's hard to get rid of, don't buy it.

For the materials you have now, look up the proper methods for each in advance. Some caustics can be diluted and put down the sink. ("Do as you oughter, add acid to water"—NEVER water to acid.) Organic materials can often be decomposed before they are discarded BUT the methods should be investigated thoroughly. Heavy metals (cobalt, nickel, mercury, lead, etc.) should NEVER be put into a water system or trash. Neither should weed killers. Call your local university or look up "Disposal" in your local yellow pages.

Some materials that are quite innocuous in small quantities can do extensive environmental damage when they go down the drain. One example is phosphates, found in strong detergents and plant foods. Significant quantities quickly cause eutrophication in small bodies of water, resulting in algal growth. Manure, even dog droppings, can have the same effect. Salt is another problem. Don't just dump salt down the drain. Help your school environment by encouraging minimal use of road salt.

If you grow cultures, make sure they are sterilized before disposal. Flood agar plates with chlorine bleach for a minimum of five minutes. Kill molds with disinfectant. Wrap terraria and animal bedding in plastic. You are responsible for the safety of everyone who handles the waste from your classroom, from custodial staff to trash collectors, as well as anyone who may use your classroom or preparation area after your activities.

Don't keep preserved specimens for more than a year. Molds grow even in preservatives. Don't keep formaldehyde in the classroom. If you have formaldehyde or specimens preserved in formaldehyde from years ago, you cannot simply throw these materials away or dump the fluids down the sink. They are considered hazardous wastes and must be handled as such.

Even the disposal of equipment can be problematic. You need a special container for "sharps"—that includes broken glass and metal pieces. Instruments containing mercury must be handled as hazardous waste.

Know the district policies and procedures for the handling of body fluids. (See Chapter 10, **Standard Precautions**.) Don't put anyone else at risk because they don't know what these are. All adults should be thoroughly knowledgeable and prepared to use Standard Precautions, and children should be given an abbreviated set of rules that is consistent with these. (See hazards symbols in Chapter 3, **Signs and Symbols**.)

Your Second Home

Good storage and safe disposal procedures are even more important for you as an employee than for your students. Occupational Safety and Health Administration (OSHA) rules were meant to protect workers who spend the majority of their day in one environment. Long-term exposure to heavy metals, formaldehyde, and other items found in some science classrooms has been associated with a variety of medical problems. Make sure your preparation space is well lit and well ventilated. Clear out everything that is unneeded or hazardous. Keep your second home as safe and secure as your primary residence.

Connections

▶ Flinn Scientific Catalog and website: *www.flinnsci.com*
▶ A good site for most chemicals: *siri.uvm.edu/msds*
▶ Links to most manufacturers' sites: *www.msdsprovider.net/Site/msdsprovider.nsf/about*

4

THE SAVVY SCIENCE TEACHER

Mr. Huang teaches science scientifically and has an exciting investigation-based program. Mr. Huang's inventory is kept on 3 x 5 cards in a recipe box. Each one has a reduced version of the MSDS warnings on the back. The cards are color-coded: red means flammable, goldenrod means corrosive, and blue means material that is quickly outdated.

Mr. Huang's locked cabinets are color-coded just like the cards. Each cabinet has the universal symbol for the chemical group on it in the appropriate color. The keys have a little colored tape on them so he can find them quickly.

The supply cabinet where equipment such as droppers, scissors, markers, and plastic dishes are kept is usually open. That's because the kids rotate responsibilities for cleaning and putting away those supplies. There's a picture of what the cabinet looks like full on the inside of the door.

Sure, the system took some time and effort to set up. But now that it's in place, adding new items is easy. As soon as Mr. Huang places his order, he has students help create the labels and index cards. Then when the items arrive, Mr. Huang just has to pull out the prepared information, complete the index card with the MSDS form, put the labels on, and put the item in its place.

Lively Science

Greg came home from school visibly upset. In class, his eyes itched and his nose was always wet. He told his mom, "I'm allergic to the teacher." It took the school nurse to discover that it wasn't the teacher that Greg was reacting to, but the teacher's classroom plants and animals.

The Living Earth

Gregor Mendel, Charles Darwin, Barbara McClintock, and Stephen J. Gould were drawn to science by living things. Despite their diverse fields, each shared a fascination with living organisms and their life cycles. Barbara McClintock called it "a feeling for the organism." That fascination pulled them irresistibly toward science. Would they have been inspired today? All too often, the part of life science that is most conspicuously absent in classrooms is the life. Living things belong in classrooms—with the appropriate cautions.

Twenty years ago, biology lessons were characterized by rows of specimens, stuffed or floating in formaldehyde. Today we have evidence that specimens carry molds and pathogens and that formaldehyde is a carcinogen, so most of the specimen jars should be gone. And today, at the elementary and middle school levels, we call the subject "life science" so we need to find techniques for bringing living organisms into classrooms that are safe for both organisms and humans.

Maintaining living things in a classroom requires knowledge and preparation. It also requires the proper equipment and space. There are two primary goals in the study of living things: first, we want our students to respect life, and second, we want them to appreciate its complexity in nature. Observing healthy living things in school accomplishes both goals. Watching organisms wither, suffer, or even die from neglect is bad education.

5

SCI LINKS
THE WORLD'S A CLICK AWAY

Topic: McClintock
Go to: *www.scilinks.org*
Code: SEL04

Selecting Organisms for Your Classroom

Like selecting a pet, selecting a classroom organism requires a realistic appraisal of your situation and knowledge of your local district policy. How much space do you have? How much time can you give? How much control do you have? Is your room shared or all yours? Will your students assume responsibility? Do any students have special needs?

Factors to Consider

Type of Organism	Level of Care	Potential Problems
Plants	Low: need light and water, can be left for vacations	▶ Molds bother some sensitive students ▶ Some plants are toxic
Aquarium fish, protists	Low: can be left for vacations	▶ Slight risk from bacteria in tank ▶ Temperature controls may be required during vacations
Crustacea and snails	Moderate: simple foods, intolerant of heat	▶ Moderate risk of bacterial contamination
Insects, butterflies	Moderate: cultures can become moldy	▶ Stings ▶ Exotic species endanger the environment
Reptiles (snakes, lizards, turtles)	High: require live food, intolerant of cold	▶ Bites ▶ Salmonella infections ▶ Moldy food ▶ Sensitive to temperature change
Rodents and rabbits	High: can't be left unattended during vacations	▶ Allergenic dander ▶ Odor from droppings and bedding ▶ Bites and scratches ▶ Human disease carriers

Alive and Satisfied

Many teachers keep classroom animals that are attractive and highly motivational. Unfortunately, other classroom menageries are risky and model poor care. The key difference is thought and preparation. Classroom organisms should teach both life science and humane treatment, not make headlines.

You need to fully understand the care requirements for any organism you bring to your classroom, as well as the allergenic and disease hazards they can pose. Consider the special needs and sensitivities of all your students as well.

- Are there allergies to dander, molds, or materials contained in the animal's food and bedding?

- Can you sufficiently monitor and control the behavior of your students to ensure that the organisms would not be harmed?

- Do you have plans in place to ensure that the animals are fed and their environments are cleaned as frequently as health and sanitation require—even when you are absent?

- Have you taken appropriate steps to prevent unwanted procreation of classroom animals?

- And should they arrive, what would you do with the progeny?

- Have you got a complete plan for the safe care of the organisms during weekends and vacations?

- What will happen to the animals at the end of the school year?

- Are you prepared to deal with the death of a classroom animal?

The educational opportunities offered by keeping living organisms in your classroom make it well worth the work and responsibility required to maintain them safely, if they are chosen with care. Let's take a closer look at some of the species that are commonly chosen as classroom creatures.

Topic: bacteria
Go to: *www.scilinks.org*
Code: SEL05

Bacterial Cultures

There are still textbooks in use that suggest students culture and study bacteria. Some outdated texts may even suggest that students culture their own bacteria by touching agar plates or culturing scrapings from the mouth or under the fingernails. This should never be done. Infectious *streptococcus* and *staphylococcus* are almost always present within the population in your classroom. If you accidentally culture these organisms, you could produce a major strep or staph outbreak with disastrous results. Even culturing vendor-supplied bacteria is not recommended at the elementary level. The danger of accidental contamination with human infectious agents is too great to warrant the risk. This is one topic where technology—photos and video clips—may be a preferred alternative to an actual classroom culture.

If you must show bacterial cultures or decide to grow molds, buy stock cultures and make sure that the container is completely sealed. Do not pass culture dishes around to students, and do not open the sealed container for a closer look.

Topic: Protista
Go to: *www.scilinks.org*
Code: SEL06

Topic: Fungi
Go to: *www.scilinks.org*
Code: SEL07

Protists

Protists have their own kingdom and their own fascination. *Amoebae, Paramecia*, and *Euglena* can teach students a lot about diversity. You will need a compound microscope that provides 100x magnification. If you bring pond water to class, know your water source and never use contaminated or polluted sources. Remind students to wash their hands immediately following the activity and to never eat in the classroom.

Be aware that some of the most dangerous water-borne diseases are caused by protists. *Cryptosporidium parvum,* found in school fountains and pools, is a parasite that causes diarrhea. There are other protists that cause intestinal diseases such as dysentery. The study of protists presents a good opportunity to remind students about the importance of hygiene, hand washing, and modern methods of water treatment.

Fungi

The kingdom Fungi includes molds, mildews, yeast, and mushrooms. Most are unwanted visitors in classrooms because of their persistence and tendency to cause allergic reactions. The first rule for fungi culture is usually "Don't." Instead, search your classroom for things that can breed molds and mildews and clean them up. That includes old carpeting and mats; animal bedding and litter; germinating seeds; plant soils taken directly from outside; and artifacts stuffed into student cubbies, desks, and lockers.

In the rare case that you want to show molds to students, keep the exercise short, specific, and contained. You can grow bread mold on homemade white bread or have students photograph things that get "green" in their home refrigerators, but keep the specimens in sealed containers when showing them. Immediately after the activity, disinfect the samples and follow with proper disposal. Make sure that custodians and service personnel are never exposed to discarded live cultures.

Never bring in mushrooms or other fungi from the wild. You can get safe mushrooms for study from the grocery store or mushroom-growing kits from supply houses for interesting lessons.

Yeasts make outstanding subjects for life science experiments. Remember, if you are preparing a yeast product for eventual consumption, do it in a kitchen, cafeteria, or home economics room—not in areas designated for science activities.

Plants

Plants are attractive, easy to maintain, and provide valuable, timely lessons. There are, however, some areas of caution.

- Some common plants or parts of plants are toxic if eaten (e.g., alamanda, oleander, hemlock, poinsettias, dieffenbachia, and holly berries).

- Some plants with edible parts have parts that are inedible and quite toxic (e.g., potato leaves and rhubarb leaves).

- Be explicit. Warn your students not to taste any plants or parts of plants in your classroom, at field sites, or even in their home gardens or yards unless the plants have been specifically grown for food—and then only the parts that are edible.

- Some plants can cause itching and blistering on contact. The most common of these are members of the *Rhus* family, commonly known as poison ivy, poison oak, and poison sumac.

- Some plants produce toxic fumes when burned. These include the *Rhus* plants and oleander. Be certain to avoid burning these materials to get rid of them, or using them as kindling or firewood.

Some Common Toxic Plants

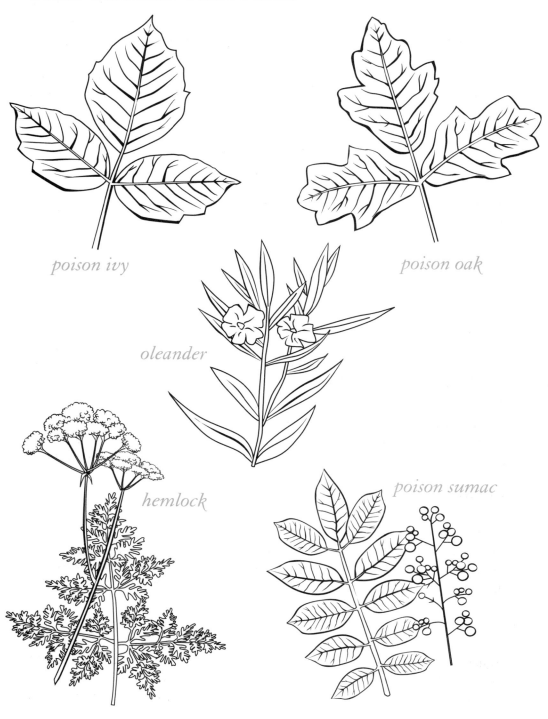

poison ivy

poison oak

oleander

hemlock

poison sumac

Be aware that unwanted molds can grow along with seeds or on plant potting soil. Treat seeds with a solution of 1% chlorine bleach for an hour before using them for student studies. Use sterilized potting soil indoors, not soil dug up from outside. Don't keep too many plants. A rain forest environment may be created in a green house but not in a regular classroom.

If you have access to a schoolyard nature area or garden, try to use native plants rather than risk bringing in plants that do not grow well in your local environment or that compete with native species. Remind younger students never to taste plants and to wash their hands after gardening.

Invertebrates

While furry animals may seem more appealing, 97% of animal species don't have backbones. For behavioral and life-cycle studies, invertebrates make good choices. They are relatively easy to maintain, they're usually inexpensive, and they reproduce quickly. Because their metabolism is different from ours, they are less likely to carry diseases that can spread to humans.

Arthropods such as insects, spiders, and crustaceans are invertebrates with external skeletons. Large populations of fruit flies, mealworms, pill bugs, ants, and dermestid beetles can be raised easily in jars or small terraria. *Daphnia* and brine shrimp are aquatic invertebrates that are barely visible to the eye. Their heartbeats can be studied under various conditions with a very low power microscope. Giant cockroaches, isopods, and hermit crabs don't take up much space. Their food is usually easy to obtain: dried fruit, plants, and grains.

But invertebrates aren't necessarily safe just because they are small. The main danger with insects is stinging. The bites of bees, wasps, and fire ants can be very painful and sometimes fatal. Most schools keep an EpiPen available to trained staff for children identified as hypoallergic. (See Chapter 10, **First Aid.**) Crabs can pinch though the pinch may be more frightening than the actual injury inflicted.

Be mindful of molds in insect terraria. And those dried bananas and apples can breed fungi that cause sneezes. Once mold gets into your classroom, it may be difficult or very costly to remove.

SCI*LINKS*.
THE WORLD'S A CLICK AWAY

Topic: invertebrates
Go to: *www.scilinks.org*
Code: SEL08

Fish

Aquarium fish are common and convenient pets. They can be maintained safely with a few commonsense precautions. Like all classroom animals, fish should come from a reputable dealer. You don't want exotic species brought directly from another country.

Resist the temptation to bring excitement into your classroom in the form of notorious species such as piranhas, large Oscar fish, and live sharks—the risk and liability are not justifiable. And remind students about hand-washing hygiene.

Regular cleaning and maintenance of the aquarium is necessary to avoid the breeding of unwanted protists and bacteria. Remember also that heat and air conditioning in your building may be turned off during weekends or extended vacations. Aquaria species may not be able to survive the temperature change.

Reptiles

Many teachers find small reptiles very convenient classroom pets because they provide a lot of opportunities for observation and can tolerate infrequent feedings. But even small reptiles require high security and caution.

Nonpoisonous snakes bite. Even some species that people don't expect to bite, such as garter snakes, do. Nonpoisonous snakes may have secretions that can cause serious effects in sensitive people. Small lizards and geckos can be good substitutes, but a few do bite. You'll need a reliable supply of food—many teachers maintain a culture of live crickets for this purpose. You should be aware that snakes and lizards seem to attract theft and vandalism more than many other classroom objects, so take appropriate steps to secure these animals.

Reptiles do not generate their own heat and self-regulate body temperature as mammals do, so you need to be particularly cautious about ensuring that the temperature of their environment is maintained. This may require the use of heat lamps and other devices.

Birds

Hint:
When teaching food webs, don't forget to add ticks and mites on the mammals and birds. This will help students understand precautions.

Birds bred by legitimate breeders are generally free from zoonotic diseases that can be transmitted to humans. But every year there are a few reported cases of disease transmitted by birds brought into the country illegally. Duck and goose droppings and unsterilized owl pellets may also carry human infectious agents. Only keep birds in the classroom if you are sure they are from a reliable source and you are prepared for constant upkeep.

Never bring a bird—alive or dead—into your classroom from the wild. They can carry ticks and other infectious, disease-causing agents. Wild birds are also protected by federal, state, and local regulations; endangered species acts; and other prohibitions.

Birds can bite and scratch, and their cages can become moldy or insect-infected. However, the chief danger in keeping birds is to the animals themselves—they are fragile and need a calm environment with a constant temperature. You must keep your classroom secure at all times.

Mammals

Resist the lure of big eyes and a furry body—unless you are very sure that you have a healthy, calm animal and that you are ready for a lot of work. Mammals are probably the least practical of classroom pets. Because other mammals bear a close species relationship to humans, they also carry more human infectious diseases.

Call of the Wild

Do not bring wild or feral animals—dead or alive—into your classroom. They
▶ may be sick, diseased, or hurt
▶ can carry a variety of infectious agents
▶ may be protected by federal, state, and local regulations
▶ require special licensing
▶ are likely to be much more aggressive than domesticated animals

5

With enough time, space, and facilities, healthy gerbils or white mice make the best classroom mammals. If you have more than one of a kind, make sure they are the same sex to avoid an exploding population. Make sure you purchase animals from a reputable pet store to ensure that they do not carry disease. Get animals accustomed to being handled by working with them yourself before you allow any students near them. And be prepared for constant vigilance; don't leave your classroom unlocked or your pets unattended. Kidnapped mice aren't a joke.

Rabbits, hamsters, and guinea pigs are much less reliable pets. When frightened, they are prone to scratch. Even when purchased from reliable sources, they often carry or contract diseases. Mammals have a protein dander under their skin that is a strong allergen to many students. This protein can't be washed or vacuumed away and can remain in a classroom for many years.

Mold breeds in wet litter. Some schools have had to completely remove classroom carpets for allergic students and employees, even though the culprit creature hasn't been there for years.

Never bring an animal that came from the wild into a classroom. They can carry zoonotic diseases such as rabies, leptospirosis (rabbits), hantavirus, and even plague (rodents). Parasites may spread to domestic animals and humans. If you or your students see an injured animal, call your state department of natural resources or county animal control officer for help but do not touch or go near the animal.

Do not bring the body of a dead animal into a classroom. Rabies is carried in the saliva of animals. Dead

SCI*LINKS.*
THE WORLD'S A CLICK AWAY

Topic: viruses
Go to: *www.scilinks.org*
Code: SEL09

animals have persistent ticks, molds, and other parasites. A mold infestation can last years in the air of a classroom. Viral and bacterial diseases can be spread by dead animals, even many days after they die. Bleach bones before bringing them to the classroom.

Escape!

Your obligation for safety doesn't stop at the classroom door. Your responsibility extends to other members of the school community and to the environment around you. This is especially important when you are maintaining living organisms. Think about disposal safety every day. Have a plan for animal wastes and litter, and share that plan with the custodian.

Make sure that you are prepared to prevent your classroom organisms from going AWOL. You need a security plan for nights and weekends. Your custodian won't want to know your pet boa has moved into the walls!

There are serious environmental consequences when exotic (non-native) animals and plants move into new environments. Kudzu, purple loosestrife, and Russian thistle are all plants that worked well in their native habitats but are wreaking havoc in new places today. Someone loved zebra mussels and English sparrows back in their original homes, but they have multiplied unchecked in new environments. So too, plants from a student's vacation can cause serious problems back home.

We often think we are being nature-conscious when we are actually causing serious problems. Popular classroom activities involving hatching and raising butterflies resulted in thousands of the insects being released into new environments. As a result, native species were endangered because of imbalances in the food chain and because some insects sold commercially are diseased. Hatching and feeding mallard ducks and Canada geese can domesticate them to such an extent that they don't take their normal fall trips south. Think about its release before you begin culturing an animal in your classroom.

In the Life Science Supply Closet

Life science activities can involve as many toxic materials and chemicals as do chemistry activities. As our understanding of toxicity increases, we must eliminate many of the chemicals that were common in earlier activities. If you inherited any of the following chemicals from prior or upper-grade teachers, contact a reliable disposal firm:

▷ Hematoxylin (a tissue stain)

▷ Toluene (used for embedding samples)

- Ethers (used for chromatography or for anesthetizing insects)

- Heavy metals (such as elemental mercury or chromium compounds commonly found in stains and metallic salts)

- Carbon tetrachloride (a once commonly used solvent)

While some firms still pack specimens in formaldehyde, it is not recommended. Because prolonged exposure to this chemical can cause cancer, ask for a substitute preservative.

For other reagents, follow the storage rules in Chapter 4. Make sure the storeroom is secure and the sections for combustibles, corrosives, and organics are separate. Do not order stronger reagents than you need. Do not accept leftover chemicals from parents, upper-grade teachers, or any source other than regular science supply vendors. (See Chapters 4 and 6.)

A Feeling for the Organism

Despite the problems and the precautions, living classroom creatures are a vital part of science education. Observing the behavior of living organisms provides rich science experiences for children at all ages. As you plan for safe and sensitive experiences with organisms, don't forget the schoolyard. Nature areas, gardens, and bird and animal feeders are recommended for students of all ages. Even in urban settings, look for mini-biomes in tree pits, parks, and cracks and crevices in sidewalks and buildings.

Young children are apt to bring living things into the classroom spontaneously—woolly bear caterpillars, slugs, earthworms, and such—which were found during the walk to school or at recess in the school yard. Try not to discourage their enthusiasm, but discuss careful handling, hand washing, and the need to return living creatures to their natural habitat. While students should never be encouraged to experiment on organisms, they can learn science and safety by doing science with organisms under your care. It's just as important to be confident and caring in the natural world as to be concerned. Make sure that every safety rule is tempered with common sense and organized planning.

Housecleaning in Life Science

There are special cleaning requirements for a lively science room:

- Make sure you always have a supply of liquid soap, paper towels, and hot water for hand washing and hygiene.
- Clean desks and counters with soap and disinfectant following life science activities.
- Remember, stains *stain*. Use minimal quantities and learn how to neutralize spills in advance.
- Have a special disposal site for biological waste.
- Do not use pesticide sprays without proper preparation and notification of parents.

5

THE SAVVY SCIENCE TEACHER

Maria K. begins her classroom cultures by asking groups of students to research the habitat needs of simple, inexpensive animals. Mealworms, guppies, crickets, and *Daphnia* are all relatively easy to culture. Local invertebrates are almost always available in a bait shop for loose change; those organisms won't present problems if they are released back into the environment.

Once a group of students has demonstrated that they know how to maintain their organism, they are given the responsibility of culture for a limited period of time. During this time they make quantitative observations of the living organism, resulting in a report or a presentation. Their studies of behavior are called ethograms. By October, Maria's students are ready to develop a display of "Creepy Creatures," which they share with the primary students around Halloween. Then, to show proper respect for the organisms, Maria's lesson ends with their release back into the wild or into a larger aquarium/terrarium setting for long-term maintenance.

Rules for Our Nature Center

- Never eat plants from outside.
- Never pet or feed wild animals.
- Report any scratches or stings.
- Wash your hands after gardening.
- Leave animal parts alone.

Pets from Home

Be cautious about inviting your students to bring their pets to school.

They may get nervous and scratch or bite when brought into your classroom.

Modern Alchemy

It's inevitable. You're grabbing milk at the corner store and a student hails you. "When we study science this year, will we get to blow things up?" Modern technology and the media have blurred the distinction between special-effect images and the real world. Teachers are challenged to communicate the excitement of the natural world in dramatic—yet safe—ways.

Science Is a State of Mind

Today's students have contact with many more complex chemicals in their homes than ever before but they may have little awareness of the physical and chemical properties of those materials. This is a situation that can be extremely hazardous. Children—even very young children—are sometimes left unsupervised at home with all these tempting hazards. Not only is chemical safety important in your school curriculum, it may also be of vital importance in ensuring safety at home.

Much of what students think they know about chemistry may be based on images they have acquired from the media. Dirty lab coats, cluttered benches, and explosions may be gone from modern research and industry but they still live on in movies, videos, and MTV. Your curriculum will compete with these images. But the good news is that the best chemical explorations are often the safest. You can—and should—provide your students with carefully planned observations of chemical phenomena that through their very simplicity are fascinating, as well as safe, and allow even very young students to control and manipulate chemical change.

Common Student Chemistry Misconceptions

- Students often believe that atoms and molecules are much larger than they are—just below visibility.
- Students find it difficult to believe that most of an atom is empty space.
- Students often can't visualize that a substance dissolves in the empty spaces among solute molecules.
- The subtle energy exchanges in common chemical reactions, taking heat in or releasing heat, are difficult to explain. Students find it difficult to believe that common chemicals can produce heat.

6

Pop, Bang, Fizz

Risking student safety with explosive demonstrations was never a good idea. So compete at a different level. Give students the opportunity to directly observe a chemical system that is simple and safe enough for them to manipulate by themselves, and forgo the urge to produce a bang. You can't possibly match the technological wonders of special-effects photography anyway. Far more impressive may be a pop or a fizz that the child can observe up close and learn to control.

Familiar Substances

Students learn best when their education is rooted in the familiar. Curriculum developers often use the word "authentic" to describe such experiences. The best way to encourage students to construct authentic and long-lasting understandings about the chemical world is to encourage careful observation. That occurs when chemical explorations use familiar substances in small quantities and are observed by disciplined students using secure equipment. There is no compromise needed between safety and science here. Observing a phenomenon in a less dramatic way requires better science skills and has a more lasting effect. When you are searching for a hands-on experience for students, begin in the kitchen or grocery store.

▶ To show that chemical reactions release heat, consider vinegar and baking soda or dissolving salts rather than stronger acids and bases.

▶ When doing acid and base studies, use carbonated beverages, lemon juice, vinegar, liquid hand soap, and baking soda.

▶ For indicators, try tea, beet juice, or red cabbage juice rather than phenolphthalein.

▶ To look at organic molecules, stick to foods such as sugars and starches.

▶ To demonstrate solubility, try table salt, sugar, starch, and powdered drink mixes.

▶ Pollution studies can be carried out with silt, clay, powdered milk, or ice melt.

Every chemical that comes into the classroom should have an MSDS with it. (For a detailed explanation of these documents, see Chapter 4.) If you have trouble getting all the information you need about a familiar product, look at the Vermont SIRI site on the Web. (See **Connections.**) Do not ask students to bring products from home to school. You cannot be certain of the selection, the contents, and the packaging of the materials your students may be contributing. Nor do you want to take the responsibility for the transport and possible misuse of these items in transit from home to your classroom.

Think Small

Even when you are using familiar substances, accidents can occur. In even the most disciplined room, someone might decide to taste something. Using the smallest possible quantity of a reagent is not only a good safe practice, it encourages students to work carefully and observe closely. Think drops rather than test tubes or cups full. With solids, think in granules and pea-sized proportions.

The "stock" supply of any chemical (even those you think are harmless) should always remain in a locked cabinet or storeroom. Before class, measure out appropriate quantities of what you will need on small squares of paper. Make sure all samples are labeled. Cafeteria trays are handy for transporting these supplies to the room when they are needed. Do not have students working in storerooms or teacher preparation areas.

Spend some time with students explaining why they need to sit still, avoid spills, and prevent contamination of the chemicals you provide. It is best to make sure everyone is seated and listening before distributing supplies and equipment. In some cases, it may be even better to have students stand since laps make big targets for even little spills. Many teachers have students write down what they are going to do—including precautions—rather than starting a science activity immediately after students return from recess. This also helps you review procedures for students who might have been absent for the first presentation of safety precautions.

Toxicity is a relative rather than an absolute characteristic. Some of the simplest chemicals can be toxic to some individuals after a single (acute) or many small (chronic) exposures. Many common household

A Sample Elementary Science Inventory

- Antacid tablets
- Baking soda
- Baking powder
- Bromthymol blue (powdered)
- Clay (potter's)
- Glucose test strips (for sugar)
- Iron filings
- Isopropyl (rubbing) alcohol
- Limestone chips
- Methylene blue stain
- pH (hydrion) paper
- Salt (rock, kosher, and reagent)
- Starch (powdered)
- Sugar
- Vinegar (white)

6

chemicals such as rubbing alcohol, bleach, and cleaning supplies are highly toxic. Be aware that exposure via absorption of fumes through the skin and mucous membranes may be far greater than by direct touching. Minimizing the time of exposure (and time in which students might get bored and begin to play) is important. Chronic exposure is most dangerous to you, the teacher.

Sample Toxicity Levels of Common Chemicals

Chemical	Animal LD50*	150 lb Adult	Effect
Mercuric chloride	5 mg/kg	‹7 drops	extremely toxic
Potassium cyanide	50 mg/kg	‹1 tsp	highly toxic
Formaldehyde	500 mg/kg	‹1 ounce	moderately toxic
Aspirin	5 g/kg	›1 ounce	slightly toxic
Table salt	3g/kg	›1 ounce	mildly toxic
Glycerin	›5 g/kg	›1 pint	nontoxic

*Amount lethal to 50% of subjects in a test within a set time

Source: *Toxicities adapted from Flinn Catalog (1999).*

Tools of the Trade

In keeping with the idea that simpler and smaller is better, you should look over your inventory of science equipment. Some of what you own may be more hazardous and less useful than their newer counterparts.

Temperature: Though teachers may be familiar with the classic glass thermometers for measuring temperature, most elementary students have never seen one. Health care professionals and parents are much more likely to use electronic probes or microencapsulated liquid-crystal tapes to measure the temperatures of sick kids. They are much safer and easier to use. Probes that can send data directly to a computer or graphing calculator can be purchased relatively inexpensively and can be shared among several teachers.

Mass: At the elementary level, pan balances reinforce the idea of measuring objects by comparing them to other objects. Simple, sturdy pan balances can be purchased economically, but you may also find it interesting to have students make their own balancing instruments.

Volume: Glass measuring containers pose an unnecessary hazard for elementary students. Plastic measuring cups with both metric and English measures are readily available in grocery and kitchen implement stores. Small-dose measuring cups can be obtained from drug stores or saved from children's cough syrup and liquid analgesic packages.

Linear Measure: Wooden meter sticks are tempting medieval weapons for some students. They can splinter. Buy flexible plastic when possible.

Sharp Instruments: Cutting tools such as razor blades and scalpels are generally not appropriate for use with young children. If you do choose to have students cut, use a blade with a safety shield and teach proper technique first. Have adults prepare materials ahead of time.

Eyewear: Almost every chemistry experiment requires safety eyewear. You need chemical splash goggles. The appropriate models are marked with a code Z87, a voluntary standard of the safety industry, and may be available in striking fluorescent colors. Eyeglasses or plastic shields—also called "plant visitor specs"—are not appropriate. You'll have to be prepared to sanitize them. If you don't have a sanitizer, 10% household bleach can be used. Be a good role model and insist on eye protection for all adults in the room as well.

Mercury-Filled Instruments

If you still have mercury-filled thermometers and barometers (the column is silver in color), you need to arrange for safe disposal of these instruments. The hazard posed by spilled mercury from broken instruments is serious and unacceptable.

For elementary classes, it may be best to avoid glass thermometers altogether, including the ones filled with red-dyed alcohol. Most students are more familiar with the electronic probes used by their pediatricians or the liquid crystal strips that change color at different temperatures.

6

Consider purchasing a demonstration ("Flex") video camera or a digital video. It can be used to record some activity that may be too small or too dangerous for students to observe closely. An instant replay of an experiment can be very valuable to student understanding. A video may also be used effectively to update students who are absent for the original activity. (See in Chapter 3, **A Basic Science Equipment List.**)

Attitude Is Everything

Scientists are made, not born. In order to get the most out of chemistry activities, students need self-discipline. Good habits are learned in small increments. Begin with short (five-minute) experiences with specific directions. Have students rate one another on their safety habits. Gradually expand the experiences and the degree of freedom you give students for good judgment. Although students should be made responsible for helping to distribute and collect supplies and equipment, do not permit them to dispense chemicals or to handle dangerous or delicate equipment and supplies.

THE INEVITABLE QUESTION

An inevitable question that emerges from chemistry activities is, "What happens when you mix...?" You must temper your reply to ensure that students understand they must not randomly mix chemicals together.

This is one circumstance when you should not encourage or permit unsupervised and undirected experimentation. Learning by doing has a powerful place in the study of science but not in the discipline of chemistry.

Students must understand in unequivocal terms that they must never mix chemicals together unless a knowledgeable adult is present and explicitly gives them permission to make the specific mixture.

Reactions that Release Heat

Try 5 mL of the first reagent in the second to show students that reactions can be dangerous:

▶ Baking soda in vinegar
▶ Effervescent antacid in water
▶ Ice melt and water
▶ Yeast in sugar water or dough
▶ A little powdered bathroom cleanser (such as Ajax) in water

Things That Go Boom

Begin with familiar chemicals in very small quantities. Show students that energy is released when some chemicals react. (See the list of possible reactions below, but keep the quantities very small and remember that everyone must use eye protection.) The reactions involve a very slight release of heat, so consider using a temperature probe to enable students to see the first results of an exothermic reaction in a safe environment. Then explore ideas; if a little of this chemical reaction causes a little heat, what might a lot do? Why is it dangerous to mix unknown chemicals? (Because they may release a lot of heat or gas.)

All chemical reaction experiments require eye protection. Unless the reaction is microscale and you are sure it cannot escape the container, consider heavy aprons and shields. For demonstrations, you can borrow appropriate safety equipment from the secondary school. That way you can be a good role model. Instilling a healthy respect for chemical reactions is an important goal of elementary chemistry education.

A LESSON IN MATERIALS SAFETY

In this lesson students become active scientists as they search and identify potentially dangerous chemicals in their schools and homes.

Activities:

▷ Introduce acids and bases with a special "breakfast" lesson in the cafeteria. Ask students to taste a variety of drinks such as juices, vinegary salad dressing, tonic water, and coffee. Then provide cups of dark Pekoe tea and/or red cabbage juice as indicators. Each student can add 10 drops of one liquid to their indicator. Classify samples as "sour" or "bitter" (acid or base) by color and effect on indicator.

▷ To explore stronger, more hazardous chemicals, ask students to put on their eye protection and nonlatex gloves. Test bleach and aspirin with the tea or red cabbage indicator, and then with pH paper. Group household chemicals as strong acids and bases.

▷ Look at the labels of common household products and discuss the precautions that should be taken with each one. Have students note that the dangers of strong acids are similar to the dangers of strong bases. Discuss ways of keeping the chemicals secure at home.

▷ For a final project, ask students to work with their parents to create an inventory of all the cleaning supplies in their homes. Then as a thank-you gift, each student can make a refrigerator magnet with the numbers of the fire department and poison control for their homes. Glue laminated tag board onto small circle or bar magnets.

The (Not So) Sweet Smell of Success

Fumes and odors can be a great problem in an elementary room because the space is seldom as well ventilated as a properly constructed science room. In closed or crowded conditions, even slight odors can become major problems. They can also spark allergic reactions. (These are more likely with organic materials. See Chapter 5.) Finally, odors tend to excite students and may cause them to be less safe than they otherwise would be. A well-ventilated science lab has fans that can move eight times the volume of the room's air each hour. It's unlikely an older classroom will meet this standard, so you need to make sure strong odors and fumes don't occur.

Minimize odors by using small quantities. Plan smelly labs for days when the windows can be opened and prepare students in advance by teaching them the proper way to test for an odor. Consider odors as warning signs of potential danger and pay close attention.

Student wafting fumes

Modern Alchemy

With care and attention, safer labs can be both scientific and fun. But you won't wean students from anticipating pop, bang, or fizz in a single session. Plan each lesson carefully and try it in advance. Don't expect great skill or maturity from the class the first time they do a laboratory. Plan a whole year of progressively greater responsibility and your lessons will be memorable.

As mentioned in Chapter 3, do not accept donated, surplus, or discarded chemicals. This may be well meaning, but it creates too much potential for hazard and liability.

Dear High School Colleagues (or Parent):

Thanks for the thought. But we can't accept your leftover chemicals. Our needs are different, and we can't store or use your chemicals safely.

Sincerely,

Your Elementary Partner

THE SAVVY SCIENCE TEACHER

Harriet G. has her fifth grade students begin their chemistry unit with a lesson called "How small is small?" Her goals in this unit include encouraging students to appreciate the value of careful observation and to understand that the physical and chemical properties of a small sample of a substance are the same as those of larger quantities. Here are some of the activities that she does:

- Students observe crystals of halite, rock salt, kosher salt, and table salt with a hand lens. They draw each and compare the shape of large and small crystals to photos of salt crystals.

- Students dissolve a 2 g crystal of halite and 2 g of powdered salt in 20 mL samples of water. They allow their solutions to evaporate in the sun and compare the salts that remain.

- Students put 1 g of rock salt and 1 g of table salt into pond water cultures and examine the appearance of *Elodea* cells in both solutions.

When they have reached an understanding that the properties of matter don't change with the size of the sample, they are ready to begin other micro-chemistry experiences.

6

Connections

Good Sources for MSDS Information:
- Vermont SIRI. *http://hazard.com* or *siri.org*
- Fisher Scientific. *www.fishersci.com*
- Cornell University. *http://msds.pdc.cornell.edu/msdssrch.asp*

Striking Gold

The traditional image of the miner is daunting: hard hat, goggles, heavy protective clothing, even a mask. In the real world, geology is sometimes a risky business. We want our students to become apprentice geologists—but if they must wrap themselves in so many protective layers, will they ever learn to dig Earth science?

Earth-Shaking Science

The Earth and space sciences provide golden opportunities for engaging, real-world experiences. Geology and astronomy are disciplines that lend themselves to many quick and timely field trips. Possibilities for study are present in every highway road cut, any construction excavation, and after any downpour. Viewing the day and night skies is free for everyone. With careful thought and planning, you can ensure that these exciting activities are done safely. Your students will also be able to share their newfound skills when exploring with family and friends. Providing your students with safe methods will bring them a lifetime of reflective observations.

Rock and Roll

Rocks and minerals may be beautiful to look at and a delight to hold, but they are also heavy and hard. They present storage challenges and occasionally tempt rowdy students. But they are also an ideal way to begin lessons on organization and scientific record keeping. Use the rocks for counting, sorting, and classifying activities. Then use the same skills as students participate in the safe storage of your collection. Keep heavy objects on low shelves and make sure boxes and bins are not top-heavy and easily tipped.

Some rocks, such as halite and some metal ores, release salts that are potentially dangerous. Despite the fact that some geology books suggest it, rocks should never be tasted for the purpose of identification. While most rock specimens can be safely stored indefinitely on secure shelving, watch out for those that oxidize such as galena (lead); the stains can damage nearby surfaces and materials. Some ores and elements are toxic (e.g., uranium, cobalt) or combustible at room temperature (e.g., potassium, sodium, phosphorus) and should never be used in an elementary classroom.

7

Managing Equipment

Earth science equipment is usually simple and sturdy. Supplies are often available at very low cost in discount stores. A few basic precautions can make these purchases very effective investments.

- **Cutters and sharps:** For the most part, cutting implements such as single-edged razor blades, saws, and scalpels are inappropriate for elementary students. Likewise, most sharps such as needles, pointed scissors, awls, and picks are also inappropriate. If you do use cutting implements or sharps, make sure they are age-appropriate, that you provide a specific safety lesson on their use, and that you check for comprehension. Streak plates are breakable and often have extremely sharp shards because they are ceramic. If something sharp must be thrown away, make sure there is a designated disposal method that your custodian will recognize. Carefully inventory your sharps and make sure you collect them all after use. Observe standard precautions with any cut. (See **Standard Precautions** in Chapter 10.)

- **Hammers:** Earth science often requires fracturing rocks, which is not the same as randomly striking or smashing the specimen. It always requires eye protection, direct supervision, and careful selection of the appropriate specimen. The rock hammer must also be chosen with care—not just any hammer but one specifically designed for the purpose. Poorly made or improper tools can break during use and cause serious injury.

- **Glues and lacquers:** Make sure that you have MSDSs on every product you use. (See Chapter 4.) Never use "super" glues, because of the potential to damage the skin and eyes. If you are lacquering fossils or other samples, provide students only a very small quantity of the coating material in a well-ventilated area.

- **Rock saws and polishers:** These are potentially quite dangerous and can't be managed safely under most elementary classroom conditions. If one or two students work with an adult on an individual project, they should all wear eye and face protection and have a thorough background in electrical and equipment safety.

- **Heat sources:** The storage and use hazards associated with alcohol burners are sufficient to ban them from use in schools in many states. There is no compelling reason to use open flames with elementary students. Hot plates can be used, but choose those designed for school science, not ones that are marketed for cooking or other household uses. Be sure you have enough power for the hot plates you intend to use and do not use extension cords or receptacle multipliers with hot plates. At the elementary level, adults should be the ones doing the heating and handling hot materials. Students should not be seated near enough to be endangered by an accidental spill. Make sure the area that you choose for the activity is not crowded with furniture or other clutter, and emphasize good discipline.

If you use hydrochloric acid, store the stock bottle (no greater than 5M [molar] HCl) in a designated acid cabinet. Place small quantities (no more than 10 mL) in dropper bottles before class. Make sure everyone—doers and observers—wears eye protection. Rinse the specimens after testing. For elementary levels there are two safer, but not always satisfactory, alternatives. You could use vinegar rather than acid, but the vinegar doesn't fizz much on most limestone samples. Or you could purchase the correct dilution of acid, but finding a place that sells it may be difficult.

Make sure that the furniture you use is strong and sturdy enough to support the weight of your specimens and your equipment. Most Earth science activities require eye protection, so make sure you have enough for everyone, as well as a safe way to disinfect.

Kids Will Get Dirty

For elementary students, Earth science = dirt. For kids, that's the best part. But teaching them to handle soils safely has a bonus—they get a second lesson in hygiene.

Obtain your samples from a source you know. Make sure that the soils you use haven't been contaminated by animal wastes or toxins. Don't keep wet soil around more than a day or two before it is used. The ideal source is commercial potting soil, which has been heated to sterilize it.

Most soils are filled with molds, bacteria, and other pathogens. Enforce appropriate hand washing. If you are testing soils in the classroom, wash the desktops too. (Don't expose students to strong disinfectants. In most cases, liquid soap will do.) Wash hands thoroughly when the lab is done. And of course, food should never be served in a room where a lab that studies dirt has taken place.

Soil molds are very common allergens. If you are building stream tables or other erosion models, limit the lesson to a few days and then take the soil outside to dry. This will prevent undue mold contamination in the classroom, which can last for years.

Seeing Stars

Ancient humans saw the same stars our students study today and shared our fascination. Astronomy is an ideal science for teaching the skills that established our methods of science— accurate observation, careful record keeping, and the relationship of technology to human progress. With very few precautions, astronomy can provide a safe and exciting curriculum.

SC*I*LINKS.
THE WORLD'S A CLICK AWAY

Topic: astronomy
Go to: www.scilinks.org
Code: SEL10

7

First and foremost, don't ever have your students observe the Sun directly. The lens of your eye concentrates solar rays in the same way that a hand lens does. Just as you can create heat with a magnifier in the Sun, so you can burn your retina when sunlight passes directly into your eye.

Sunglasses are not a protection. Special eye protection for observing eclipses can be purchased but is generally costly. Teach students the pinhole/reflection method of observing eclipses shown below.

A pinhole projector

Some familiar astronomy activities may require extra caution. One traditional lab has students throwing small objects (such as peas) into flour or plaster of Paris to model craters. Like all projectile activities, this requires eye protection.

For economic and simple, direct, individual viewing at the elementary level, binoculars are recommended over telescopes. If you are fortunate enough to have access to telescopes that automate finding and focusing on specific objects, be sure to teach students the correct way to use and care for this particularly delicate optical instrument. If the telescope is connected to a computer, make sure that the electrical connections are not exposed to moisture of any kind.

Excellent Eclipse Observations

Before you begin, make sure students are well informed about the dangers of looking at direct sunlight—even in an eclipse. The shadow of a solar eclipse, however, can be observed safely through a pinhole.

Make a small hole in a piece of tag board and provide students with a second piece of white paper. Channel the image of the Sun through the small hole onto the white paper. As the eclipse approaches, the shadow of the Moon will clearly be seen moving across the reflected image of the Sun.

In the Field

The study of Earth processes can begin in the schoolyard. Just observing the playground, the school building, and the sidewalks can provide examples of erosion and weathering.

No matter how close a trip is to the classroom, remind students of the rules for proper behavior in a field study. (See Chapter 9.) Before you go, discuss the proper way to travel; prohibitions against running, jumping, and shoving; and the proper way to carry equipment. Some precautions for playground equipment are included in Chapter 8 in **Getting in the Swing**.

Geology fieldwork almost always requires some protective gear. In a mine, quarry, or on rough terrain, students must wear hard leather shoes with toe protection and ankle support. This will require some careful consideration in advance; many young children today don't own anything but athletic shoes. This may limit where you do your fieldwork. If your students are to visit any active site, you may be required to also have hard hats available. Check in advance.

Golden Opportunities

For many elementary students, the Earth and space sciences are the first real experimental investigations that they do—the first "Aha!" experiences that they take home to share with their families. In return, parents often feel comfortable reinforcing their children's new interest in geology or astronomy at home and on family vacations.

These units are ideal vehicles for sharing your concern for safety with your school community too. It's well worth the effort. Imagine your students in years to come, shooting the rapids or flying over irrigated fields, applying the knowledge you provided in your classroom and just outside the window. So dress yourself in a little common sense and dig in.

7

Connections

▶ NSTA Press. 2001. *Dig In! Hands-on Soil Investigations*, Arlington, Va. NSTA Press.

THE SAVVY SCIENCE TEACHER

Adrianne B.'s fourth grade students know a lot about dirt. They know about the mud under the swings, the silt that accumulates at the end of the drive, and the fresh topsoil that has been applied around the shrubbery by the office. They used their knowledge of dirt to help the school solve a problem—that big, ugly puddle that always shows up under the end of the slide.

To find out how to improve their playground, Adrianne's students used paint-roller pans as stream tables to investigate erosion. Then they researched the recommended surfaces for playground equipment and invited their school's insurance loss-control representative to tour their schoolyard with them. Next the students tried some new safety surfaces in their stream tables. They found that a synthetic material made of bits of recycled tires had the highest safety rating and the least erosion.

Together the fourth graders made presentations to the school board and the parent-teacher organization. As a result of their research, those groups are splitting the cost of new safety surfaces. There will be fewer scrapes and muddy shoes in fourth grade next year.

7

Falling for Science

When Galileo watched the cathedral's pendulum swing, no one feared that it would fall on anyone's head. Newton's apple wasn't sprayed with pesticides. Today's physical science should be just that simple; our students are living lessons in movement, velocity, and acceleration. Our challenge is often to slow them down enough so they can see the world (like Newton) "on the shoulders of giants."

Getting in the Swing

Many safety books focus on chemistry, the "wet" physical science. Yet most elementary curricula appropriately concentrate on physical science that is easier to see—and more developmentally appropriate. The physical sciences provide great opportunities for teachers to examine students' preconceptions and teach them to be logical. Exploring the physical world requires only a few basic precautions to ensure safety.

Many of the principles of basic mechanics developed by Galileo and Newton are as near as the school grounds. There are a number of excellent source books on the physics of toys, playground equipment, and household tools. For these lessons, safety is also the application of common sense.

Galileo studied mechanics by dropping things, and so can elementary students. Think about safety at the beginning, the middle, and the end of the experiment. Make sure that in their excitement, students cannot fall from the launch/drop point. Consider the landing area, as well as potential landing areas should the object miss its intended target. Ensure that no persons, breakable objects, or equipment can be hit by the falling object either at the landing spot or in the path from the launch to the ground.

Playground equipment can also be used to teach physical principles. New standards have been developed for such equipment nationwide. Be certain that all equipment you use meets those standards and that your proposed use of the equipment falls within the scope of its intended use. Make sure that student observing or recording activities are well outside the range of moving components such as swings. For example, on a swing set the danger area has a radius twice as great as the farthest

8

horizontal reach of the swing. Make sure that students climbing on play structures are not carrying objects that could fall on someone below or could break. Also ensure that students are not wearing clothing with loops or ties that could get entangled and trap or choke a child.

Managing Equipment

Physical science equipment ranges from simple tools to sophisticated electrical meters. Refer to the equipment section of Chapter 7 for some basics on hammers, saws, and equipment that might be used for construction projects. Here are a few other common things that might be in your curriculum:

- *Pendulums:* The safe conduct of these activities is highly dependent on class discipline. Begin with short strings and rounded bobs. Encourage careful observation and good record keeping. Teach students to begin the swing by letting go of the pendulum bob rather than pushing or throwing it with uncontrolled force.

- *Momentum carts (cars):* Be aware of the placement of ramps. Make sure they do not block walking paths or allow cars to zoom off and hit something by accident. Make sure cars aren't left out on the floor or any other walking area.

- *Carbon dioxide pellets:* These can produce significant momentum. Cars using them should be run on tracks, not freely. Eye protection is needed.

- *Model rockets:* Use only approved engines and electrical igniters. Students launching rockets must be supervised and must wear eye protection.

Sights and Sounds

Physical science includes the study of light and sound. In teaching these topics, you can instill ideas that assist students in protecting their own sight and hearing—two vital yet fragile senses.

Insist upon and model the use of eye protection at all appropriate times. This should include protection from liquid splashes, projectiles, and harmful wavelengths of light. Modern technology has made the use of laser light simple, inexpensive, and common. Your students should be taught the hazards of laser light—particularly laser pointers—and learn never to look at the light directly or point the light into the eyes. Work with children to help them understand the dangers of staring directly at any bright light, particularly the Sun. (See the explanation of the lens of the eye in the section on the Sun in Chapter 7, **Seeing Stars.**)

Light bulbs themselves pose a number of hazards. Heat generated by bulbs can cause serious burns. The bulbs are usually made of glass, so a breakage hazard is always present. Teach students to avoid handling bulbs directly, particularly halogen bulbs. Salt and oils from bare hands can cause the bulbs to shatter when turned on.

Hearing damage caused by loud and/or constant sound is a growing problem among young people. Kids use headsets, boom boxes, and other sources of loud music and sound without realizing the extent of permanent damage that can be done to their hearing. Whether you are conducting specific activities on sound or using equipment for another reason, avoid devices that generate more than 85

FORM A CADRE OF ELECTRICAL SAFETY EXPERTS

Encourage students to be safety experts at home as well as in school:

> Make sure your outlets are not broken and that plugs fit well in them.

> Never stick anything into an electrical receptacle or plugged-in appliance—use safety covers on unused receptacles when young children are present.

> Check the wattage of light bulbs and make sure they are not too large for the appliances or the wall sockets.

> Don't use multiple extension cords on the same circuit and don't cover extension cords with carpet or other floor covering.

> If an appliance trips a breaker, turn it off until the appliance is checked.

> Keep space heaters at least one meter away from walls.

> Never use an electrical appliance near water. Don't use outdoor tools in the rain.

More tips: The National Electrical Safety Foundation. *www.nesf.org/home/safety.html*

8

decibels of sound. Even at that level, the ear will accommodate by temporarily "shutting down," and students could have trouble discriminating sounds afterward.

Charge Ahead

Many physical science activities require electrical devices, either alone or interfaced to computers. Teaching students to have a healthy respect for electricity is important in school and in their daily lives.

Classrooms in older schools are notoriously short of receptacles. Don't try to solve the problem by using socket multipliers or multiple extension cords. More places to plug in does not equal more capacity. In fact, more wire produces more resistance, less usable power, and a greater fire hazard. All outlets should be properly grounded and all outlets near water should be protected with a ground-fault interrupter (GFI). If your room does not have adequate electric service, or if the outlets do not have the proper grounding and safety features, make a request for upgrade or repairs in writing and be sure to include both the educational and safety reasons for your request.

If you need power in the middle of the room, make sure the cords are taped down securely and take them back up immediately after the activity. Be sure that all electrical equipment you use is properly grounded.

Typical household (120-volt) receptacles come in three varieties. The oldest variety has two equal openings, and plugs can be inserted in any direction (Figure 1). Newer receptacles have directional current, with one slot larger than the other (Figure 2). Televisions and some other electrical devices must be plugged in one direction, not another. The third and preferred form of receptacle has two slots of different sizes and a third opening for a ground (Figure 3). This is the only form of plug that is safe in a classroom.

Figure 1   *Figure 2*   *Figure 3*

A few household and school devices require 240-volt plugs. These are generally round, with large openings arranged radially. The configuration of the 240-volt socket is matched to the amperage that the circuit can safely carry and must be followed specifically. For example, a receptacle for an electric dryer cannot be used for an electric baseboard heater. Generally in schools, the only devices that require 240-volt circuits are electric ranges and kilns.

The most power-consuming activities are those that heat or cool. So what can an inquiring teacher do if there is not enough power? Look for low-wattage appliances. Plan activities at centers or stations so that the most power-intensive work won't have to be done by everyone at the same time. When working with young children, only adults should heat materials.

Electricity follows the path of least resistance to the ground. The presence of many electrolytes makes human tissues excellent conductors, so electric shock is an ever-present danger. Do not attempt any repair or manipulation of any electrical appliance or equipment that is plugged in. When touching an active electrical appliance, use only one hand—keep the other hand at your side or in your pocket—so that in case of electric shock, the current has less chance of flowing through your entire body.

An Electrical Primer

- Electrical current is the flow of electrons.
- It is pushed by electrical potential, measured in volts. The voltage of a battery measures its push.
- Current is measured in coulombs (the charge of 6.28×10^{18} electrons). The speed of 1 coulomb is measured in amperes.
- A conductor is a material that contains mobile electrons, those that move easily. An insulator has tightly bound electrons and high resistance to current. Resistance is measured in ohms.
- Batteries produce direct current (DC). The current in wall circuits alternates (AC).

Humans are sensitive to electrical charges. The pacemaker of the heart generates a charge across the organ that makes it contract. The flow of that charge can be measured in the fingers and toes by an electrocardiogram machine. Most people can sense as few as five milliamperes of direct current. As the current increases, muscles contract and spasm, and eventually the heart and diaphragm stop. Nine milliamperes from a battery or 2 milliamperes from a wall circuit would be felt as a shock. More than 60 amperes from a battery or 9 amperes from a wall socket would cause a painful and potentially dangerous shock. Low voltages can cause severe burns even if they don't threaten life.

Even when receptacles are safe and circuits are adequate, there can still be danger. Fuzz or lint can enter sockets. Equipment can overheat and cause fires or melt internal parts. Insulation can be nicked or damaged, causing current to flow to parts of the machine where it is not intended. Check electrical equipment and power cords

8

carefully before each use. If something appears abraded or damaged, arcs, sizzles, heats up, flickers, or pops a circuit, don't use it.

Shoot for the Stars

While there are challenges in providing a good physical science program, there are many advantages too. The safety skills you teach have outstanding value in the real world of your students. You can easily enlist expert help for this project. Call your local power company for a good safety presentation or your local building inspector for expert help in providing an improvement plan. It will make your program even better.

The Computer Age

Computers have added an entirely new level of challenges to classroom design. Classrooms designed and built prior to the use of computers almost never have sufficient electrical service in needed locations. Surge protectors and universal power sources (UPS) are needed to protect valuable and sensitive computer equipment from power surges and outages.

Computers and related equipment also require additional space. They should not be placed near sinks and should be spaced far enough apart so that students can use them without interfering with other equipment and each other.

If your room isn't equipped with sufficient power in the appropriate locations for full desktop computers, consider laptops. At the elementary level, portable word-processing machines (such as Apple's Alpha Smart) may be a good alternative because they fit into a rechargeable stand. This stand can be moved to a room with adequate power for a good recharge each afternoon.

The batteries that are used for computers and calculators are usually specialized for the use and the device. If they can be recharged, follow the instructions exactly and use the supplied recharger. Do not mix these batteries with those used for science and other activities.

SC*L*INKS.
THE WORLD'S A CLICK AWAY

Topic: electricity
Go to: *www.scilinks.org*
Code: SEL11

A Classroom Electrical Safety Tour	Y/N
1. Are your cords out of the flow of traffic? (No frays, staples, taped repairs.)	
2. Are your receptacles carrying the proper load? (No multiplied sockets.)	
3. Is your circuit breaker clearly labeled and free from obstruction?	
4. Are the outlets firm, tight, and unbroken?	
5. Are appliances unplugged when not in use?	
6. Are appliances equipped with grounds?	
7. Are all the grounds being used?	
8. Are the appliances far from water?	
9. Are the circuits equipped with ground fault interrupters?	

Source: Sarquis. 2000.

Connections

▶ Sarquis, M. 2000. *Building Student Safety Habits for the Workplace.* Middletown, Oh.: Terrific Science Press.

▶ McCullough, J., and R. McCullough. 2000. *The Role of Toys in Teaching Physics.* College Park, Md.: AAPT.

8

THE SAVVY SCIENCE TEACHER

Margaret's unit on "Batteries and Bulbs" ends with a dissection! Every student is encouraged to find a nonfunctional electrical appliance and pull it apart. The students find the essential components of the device and prepare a presentation on how the energy is converted within the device. Before they begin, all students and their parents must show that they understand the rules for safety:

- Always treat electricity with respect. It can hurt or even kill a person.
- If you think your machine has a "short" or other electrical problem, don't even try to plug it in because it could shock you.
- Unplug your machines when you examine them. If they use batteries, take the batteries out.
- Recycle batteries in the proper place. The local post office may have a battery-recycling box.
- Never open a machine with a "TV" screen in it, because those machines store dangerous charges.
- Remove plugs first so that someone won't accidentally try to plug in a broken machine.
- Wear gloves if the machine has sharp parts. Sit down when you use a screwdriver.
- Place all small pieces of your machine in a safe, secure place. Only keep the pieces that tell the story of energy in and work done. Throw broken fragments away.
- If the machine contains any liquids or chemicals, call an adult to help you remove and dispose of them properly.
- If there are glass bulbs, wrap them carefully before you throw them away.

Then they research old and new devices on *www.howthingswork.com* and suggest better inventions.

8

The Great Outdoors

Ms. Lee's class walks in pairs the few blocks to Emerald Park. Mark in his wheelchair and his partner Kris lead the double line of 22 other exuberant third graders. Each student has a clipboard, pencil, and a notebook containing observations and measurements made during their fall and winter visits. Around each student's neck is a string with a hand lens and a 15 cm ruler. Each pair of students also has 4 m of string and 4 ice-cream sticks. Ms. Lee's student teacher, Mark's aide, and five parents accompany them.

The students look for the observation areas that each pair picked out during the first visit last fall. Gerri and Sanjay wonder if they have found the correct location. The 1 m tall bush that was in the middle of their plot is no longer there. So they check their maps. Upon closer examination, they find a small sawed-off stump where the bush used to be. Their adventure yields lessons in science, time, and safety.

The Limits of Your Classroom

Your own classroom is rich with resources and activities, but there are some things that simply can't be done there. Sometimes you have to go elsewhere to collect real-life data—an exhibit, some equipment, or some experience that cannot be duplicated in your school. Well-planned field trips are a vital part of the total educational program. They play an important role in helping students relate basic concepts learned in the classroom to practical work and applications in the real world. But in today's tight-budget, cost-cutting era, you need to take more time to ensure that the few resources available to support off-campus activities are used effectively. The purpose and goals of the trip need to be integrated with the learning expectations of your program. And just as importantly, the activity needs to be planned well ahead of time to ensure a safe and productive experience.

Because you will be working outside the confines of your classroom, in addition to the safety issues you would normally encounter in planning for science activities,

9

you now need to account for the fact that the venue may be larger, less familiar, and there likely will be more excitement surrounding the activity.

when planning activities outside of the classroom.

SOME THINGS TO CHECK

- What are the natural boundaries of the site?
- Are there hazards within the boundaries of the site?
- Are there hazards accessible from the site?
- Is there any toxic vegetation?
- What is the likelihood of insect hazards (e.g., deer ticks, mosquitoes, bees, spiders)?
- Are animal encounters likely?
- What are the tripping or falling hazards?
- Can you see and monitor all students at all times?
- Are there private property/trespass issues?
- Is there a chance of the presence/intrusion of other groups or individuals?
- What are the conservation restrictions?
- How much Sun exposure are students likely to get?
- Are there water hazards?
- Where are the rest room and washing facilities?
- What is the nearest emergency medical facility?
- What is the nearest source of help?
- Where is the nearest phone?

9

Low Cost—No Cost

Go outside! Even if you start out of your building

Consider making your first field study one that can be done just outside your building. This way, you can test the maturity of your students and their ability to respond to your instructions in a more open environment. You can begin training helpers to assist with monitoring the students' work and ensuring their safety in a less formal setting than your classroom.

Regardless of the location of your school, there are opportunities for field studies right outside the school building—on school grounds or very close by. A strong investigative science program depends on providing students with the opportunity to collect and analyze data. For young children, this can be as simple as counting the number of vehicles or people that pass by or observing the size and shape of shadows cast by a building or piece of equipment on school grounds. The simpler the task, the better.

When you choose a simple phenomenon to observe, it is easier to find and limit the number of variables that need to be controlled in the observations (e.g., time of day, location, measuring instrument, and technique for measuring). And by beginning with a simple field activity in a nearby, familiar location, you can also more easily observe and identify possible safety hazards.

Scout It Out and Be Prepared

As part of your lesson planning, you must thoroughly examine the site. If at all possible, every person who will be accompanying you and your students should also preview the site. Your checklist of things to do at the site should include surveying the site for possible safety hazards.

If you expect to use staff or consultants from the field site, then a full and detailed planning session should include a discussion of exactly how you will prepare your students, what you expect your partner/consultants to do with your students, and enough information about your group and individual students for the "outsider" to know what to expect and how to work safely and effectively with your class.

You must determine clearly and exactly who will be in charge of each and every student at every moment of the out-of-class activity. The greatest potential for problems arises when one adult assumes that another adult is responsible for a child or group without being certain that the other adult is in place and has explicitly recognized and accepted the responsibility.

As discussed in Chapter 1, always keep in mind that you are responsible for everything that is done with your class at all times. That is key to recognizing the steps you need to take in preparing for a field trip. Even though there are extra adults, remember it is also your responsibility to thoroughly prepare your assistants for their duties.

Do not invite or accept any other person's assistance in your class and with your students unless you have personally reviewed the entire plan, purpose, and procedure for the activity. A few quick comments five minutes before the activity begins are not enough. Remember, most parents have not supervised more than a half dozen young children at any one time. What you do every day out of habit is not necessarily second nature or inherently obvious to even the most responsible parent, student teacher, or aide. Think of the many things that you have learned the hard way and make sure

9

your volunteers do not do the same! And if you do use parents as chaperones, be sure that they do not bring younger siblings or any other guests along.

HOW MANY IS ENOUGH?

There is no clear ratio of adults to students that can be applied to fieldwork. The right number depends on such disparate factors as the distance and location of the site, the hazards at the site, the nature of the activities you have planned, the skill and experience of the chaperones, and the behavior of the students in your class. However, here are some guidelines to help:

- Do not count yourself in the adult/student ratio or assign yourself to a specific group—you need to be available to monitor the overall activity and support your helpers.

- Special education aides should not be counted in the adult/student ratio. In groups with special education students, the aide(s) should be in addition to the sub-group chaperone.

- Every child in a chaperone's group should be clearly visible and reachable by the chaperone at all times.

- Include enough adults to allow one or more adults to go for help or stay with an injured student while still having enough adults to properly supervise the remaining students.

- Make sure you conform to any adult/student policies required by school authorities.

How Are You Going to Get There?

9

The buddy system is a must for any off-site activity. Even if you are asking students to work in small groups, it is critical that every student be specifically paired with one other student who must always be aware of what is happening to the buddy. It is just too easy for even a group of three or four to get so engaged in some task or discovery that one missing member might not be noticed immediately. Make sure that all students know who their buddies are, who else is in their group, and which chaperone has been assigned to their group.

Walking may be the best and most convenient way of reaching an outdoor site. It gives you the greatest flexibility and the lowest cost. Be sure you review crossing and waiting rules, especially if you are anywhere near roadways, driveways, bike paths, or other hazardous crossings. You will need an adult at the beginning and at the end of the group. As a general rule, put your slowest walkers at the front and the quickest at the back. The slowest walkers should set the pace.

Public transportation (buses, trains, trams, trolleys, subways, ferries) may be available to you. If so, this may be an economical option, as well as an opportunity to teach your students how to use public transportation safely and responsibly. If you use public transportation, remember that it may be more difficult to get a group on and off the vehicle during scheduled stops than if you were traveling alone. So make sure you review the embarkation and disembarkation instructions carefully with students and chaperones. You do not want an individual or equipment left behind on a vehicle or a platform.

A school bus or chartered bus is the most common method of transporting students to and from field sites. To ensure you get to the correct place at the right time and return as expected, you need to supply written plans and instructions that include:

▶ Number of adults, number of students

▶ School pick-up time

▶ Destination and drop-off location at the trip site

▶ Field site departure time

▶ School return time and pick-up location

Whether you travel on foot, or by public or private transportation, when you are off site, you and your students will most likely come into contact with people whom you don't know. It is imperative to discuss ahead of time appropriate and inappropriate interactions with "strangers." Your students must know that courteous behavior is expected but that they need to limit their conversation and contact.

A Meeting Place

Establish a specific meeting place and make that place the very first stop with all your students and chaperones.

Make sure that everyone knows when and under what circumstances to stop the activity and report immediately to the meeting place.

Accounting for Everyone

Check the total number of students and adults

▶ before leaving the classroom
▶ when beginning walking or during boarding of vehicle
▶ at least once per hour at the site
▶ prior to moving from one site to another
▶ upon arrival at each new location
▶ at every boarding of vehicle
▶ prior to departure
▶ upon return to school

9

They should never divulge personal information, accept any items, permit personal contact, or become separated from the group and assigned chaperone. Instruct students to immediately report to you or their designated chaperone if they experience any unwanted, unusual, or uncomfortable contact from anyone, including authority figures and persons in charge of the site you are visiting.

Museums, Zoos, Outdoor Education Centers, and Other Institutions and Establishments

Young children are often taken on field trips to science museums, children's museums, discovery centers, zoos, and the like (also known as informal education resources). The most productive and the safest of such visits are those with a planned and narrowly focused purpose that has been carefully discussed in advance with the educational staff of the institution to be visited.

Preparatory classroom work before the visit is also important. The greatest potential for disappointment and trouble arises when the visits are general tours, or when the teacher simply turns students over to the institution staff. Without a specific series of tasks to complete, questions to answer at the site, and objectives that are an integral part of your school program, students are easily tempted to race through the site, hide or get lost, cause disturbances, harm exhibits, and hurt themselves.

With a clear focus, they are much less likely to amuse themselves in unproductive or dangerous ways. Your presence and active participation with the institution's instructors are also imperative to ensure that students understand that the activity is very much a part of the ongoing educational plan. You are the one who knows your students best and you are responsible for knowing exactly what they have been taught and what they have experienced, even if you are not the lead instructor.

Outdoor Sites

Whether the site is as near as just outside the school doors or far enough away to require a bus or even an overnight stay, you need to check out the possible hidden hazards, especially if you are using an unfamiliar location. You should also make sure that the site does not carry restrictions for use and access (e.g., conservation land, wildlife preserve, private property, hazardous materials contamination).

We Have Met the Enemy and They Are Us

If there is a building or structure (e.g., bridge or tower) near your chosen site, you should find out if there have been refurbishing projects that could have taken lead paint off the structure and allowed lead dust to contaminate the area. If utilities have right-of-ways in or near a site, you need to be certain that high-voltage hazards are not close by. Do not count on students to read and obey "Danger, Keep Out" signs. Sites near utilities and manufacturing and research facilities should be checked for the possibility of toxic wastes. Areas formerly used for military training may contain unspent munitions.

Water, Water Everywhere

Water bodies present a number of hazards that need to be checked and carefully avoided. Remember that young children can drown in water less than 15 cm (6 in) deep. What is the footing like near the water's edge? Is the water biologically or chemically contaminated? If students are going out onto a body of water such as a lake, pond, or the ocean, you need to ensure that everyone knows the water safety rules and that you have met all the rules and regulations. Regulation life preservers should be on and not just available. Is a person trained in water rescue available? Are you and others trained in cardiopulmonary resuscitation (CPR)?

Our House Is a Very Very Very Fine House

Planning to Use Public Transportation
- Check schedules
- Contact the transportation authority to be sure they can accommodate your group with their regularly scheduled runs
- Review procedures and expectations with chaperones and students
  - Who will pay the fares
  - Where you expect to get on and off
  - What to do if someone gets separated from the group
  - Courtesy and consideration
  - Interaction with strangers

In the outdoors, it is likely that you will be intruding on the homes of large and small wild organisms. Remember, these are their homes: you and your class are the aliens. You need to be aware of insects that are indigenous to the area and whether they could carry infectious human disease (e.g., Lyme disease, encephalitis, yellow fever). Check with your district medical services if you have any questions or doubts. If you plan to use insect repellent, make sure that you check with the district medical authority as to the potential toxicity of repellents that contain DEET. Determine whether anyone on the trip has allergies to bee stings or other insect bites and what you are required to do about it.

What other animals are likely to be found at or near your site? What is the normal behavior of these animals? What are signs that the animal may be sick or injured? You do not have to be the expert on this, but you do need to check with a naturalist or guide who is familiar with the location and can advise you thoroughly and accurately. As a rule, the normal behavior of animals is to hide or run from humans. One that approaches your group or does not scurry away is more likely to be sick or injured and should be left alone and avoided. Warn children not to feed them or try to corner them. Be especially cautious of animals that may be nesting or nurturing young. An animal protecting its young is likely to be very aggressive. Above all, do not touch or approach a sick or injured animal—do not attempt a rescue or try to bring it back to your classroom.

Parsley, Sage, Rosemary, and Thyme

Vegetation in an outdoor area can also pose hazards. To begin with, nothing should be tasted or eaten. Some exceptions may be appropriate if you are working with a facility formally developed for outdoor education and with specific "wild" specimens deliberately cultivated or identified for a tasting activity. But even professional botanists will tell you that species can be confusing. Very few will *ever* eat a mushroom taken from the wild.

Pollen and spores may cause allergic responses. Be sure to check for allergic sensitivities among your students and assistants. If you have sensitive students, you may want to avoid outdoor activities altogether when pollen counts are high.

Plants can also cause serious irritation on contact. The best known are members of the *Rhus* family, commonly called poison ivy, poison oak, poison sumac, and poison elder. These plants are widespread in outdoor areas and may have different appearances in different habitats and seasons. Learn how to identify them and teach your chaperones and students to do the same. (See **Plants** illustration in Chapter 5.)

Some people mistakenly believe that they are immune to the irritants in these plants because they have come into contact with poison ivy or its relatives without developing the classic itching and blistering response. In fact, sensitivity to the antigens can develop as a result of a series of exposures, with each subsequent contact resulting in stronger response.

The saps of many plants are serious irritants, particularly milky-looking saps. Children should be taught to avoid touching plants they are unfamiliar with and to wash off thoroughly following accidental contact. Be sure to warn against rubbing of eyes that may transfer substances from the hands to the eyes.

SPF

The potency of sunscreens and blocks is measured by their Sun protective factor (SPF). Sunscreens with SPFs between 15 and 30 will block most harmful ultraviolet (UV) radiation, according to the National Cancer Institute.

If a campfire or something similar is planned, be sure you know the contents of the wood and twigs being burned. Burning such things as oleanders and *Rhus* create highly toxic fumes.

The Sun Also Rises

We now know there is reason for serious concern about skin damage caused by Sun exposure. Excessive Sun exposure when young can greatly increase the risk of skin cancers many years later. Therefore hats, long-sleeved clothing, and sunblock are necessary precautions for everyone working in the outdoors. Be sure lips and ears are also protected. Heat and dehydration are factors to be considered. Make sure the work area does not get too hot (or too cold) and that everyone remembers to drink plenty of fluids.

LIGHTNING STRIKES

Lightning is a form of electricity with extremely high voltage, produced by charges in the upper atmosphere. Lightning strikes somewhere on Earth 100 times each second, and each year about 1000 persons are killed by it. Many more persons are hurt.

Because lightning finds the best *conductor* to reach the ground, it is more likely to hit a standing human being than the flat ground around him or her.

If you can see lightning or hear thunder you are at risk: Seek shelter in a large building or an enclosed vehicle. Never stand under a tree or near a tall, projecting structure that might provide a *conducting* path for the lightning bolt to reach the ground.

Learn more about lightning hazards at: *www.azstarnet.com/anubis/zaphome.htm*

What's the Weather?

You may not be able to control the weather but you better make sure you're prepared for it. Know what the variations in temperature and weather can be at the site you choose. What are the risks of sudden storms or flooding? Make sure you know and make sure you have a shelter and evacuation plan.

Once you have obtained the information you need to fully understand the site and its potential hazards, you need to plan training for your chaperones and lessons for your students. These lessons should alert students to the hazards and give explicit instructions on how to avoid problems. These should begin before the trip and then be reviewed and enhanced at the site as closely as possible to when and where the hazard is likely to arise.

9

Equipment and Supplies

When planning for an outdoor activity, you need to think about two categories of equipment and supplies:

▶ Items needed to complete the planned activities

▶ Items needed to keep the group safe

You also need to make sure that equipment used outdoors is sturdier and less breakable than what you might use in the more controlled environment of your regular classroom. Try to avoid anything made of glass and anything that is fragile or brittle (e.g., use plastic sampling containers rather than glass, metal probes rather than glass, plastic hand lenses and water magnifiers rather than regular microscopes).

Weight and bulk should also be considered. Make student pairs or groups responsible for carrying and accounting for specific items, and then make sure that the materials are packed for safe transport and are light enough for the students to handle easily. Plan sufficient time for equipment to be returned, counted, and repacked before leaving the field site.

Dress and footwear should not be left to chance or imagination. Make sure you provide students and parents with a clear list of appropriate clothing and shoes for the outdoor adventure. Dressing in layers is a useful strategy. It allows for adjustments to be made at the site. Hats are useful in both hot and cold situations. In sunny weather, they provide shade; in cold weather, they protect from loss of body heat. Shoes need to provide good support for the arches and ankles and have nonslip soles. Open-toed shoes, sandals, thongs, and slipper-style are inappropriate for fieldwork. Extra toe protection and waterproofing is also a plus.

What to include in your first aid kit depend upon the hazards of the site. Plan your first aid kit item by item rather than generically. Make sure that you have sufficient drinking water or other beverages for the duration of the trip. As a consequence, you also need to plan for the availability of rest rooms.

Permissions

Your district or school may have a standard form permission slip. If so, you should begin with that document. However, because science field trips may entail more complexity than other field trips, make sure you include additional information that alerts parents to the nature of the activities planned and the special preparation that might have to be made (e.g., clothing requirements). Request, too, that parents make you aware of special needs that their children may have (e.g., allergies) even if they have already done so previously.

Your permission slip cannot relieve you or the school of liability for student safety. But it is an important legal document to show that you were well organized and had planned carefully.

SAMPLE HEALTH INFORMATION FORM

Source: *The Brookline Public Schools, Mass.*

For overnight, out-of-state, and out-of country field trips

Child's name _____   Date of Birth _____

Address _____   Telephone # _____

Parents/Guardians

Name _____   Work Phone # _____

Name _____   Work Phone # _____

Family Doctor _____   Telephone # _____

Emergency Contact Person (If parents/guardians not available)

Name _____   Phone # _____

Address _____   Work Phone # _____

HEALTH INFORMATION

1. Is there a PEANUT, BEE STING, or INSECT allergy?___If yes, treatment_____
_____
Any other allergies (food, aspirin, etc.)?____ What?_____ if yes, treatment _____
_____

2. Does your child have any medical condition?_____If yes, state diagnosis, treatment, medication

3. Has your child been exposed to any communicable diseases within the past 21 days? ____ If yes, specify _____

4. Is there any factor that makes it advisable for your child to follow a limited program of physical activity, i.e., heart, recent fracture or surgery, asthma, abnormal fear? _____ If yes, specify in which ways you wish his/her program limited.
_____

5. To protect your child from any possible embarrassment, does he/she wet at night?_____ sleep walk _____?

6. Please list date of the most recent tetanus shot _____

7. Is your child bringing medication, including over-the-counter and prescription? _____ If yes, complete the Medication Administration Form on the reverse side.

*Medications MUST be properly labeled in their original containers.

Parents/guardians will be contacted in case of serious sickness or accident. However, in the event of an emergency situation that requires immediate medical attention I, the parent (guardian), hereby give permission to the physician selected by the director of the trip leader in charge to hospitalize, secure proper treatment for, and to order injection, anesthesia, or surgery for my child as named above.

Signed: _____ Relationship: _____ Date: _____

SAMPLE MEDICATION ADMINISTRATION FORM

Each medication (including vitamins and supplements) must have a separate listing and complete instructions or the medication cannot be administered.

Child's name _____

1. (Medication) _____

(Dosage/How much) _____ (Frequency/How often) _____

(Diagnosis/Symptoms/What is this being administered for?) _____

_____

2. (Medication) _____

(Dosage/How much) _____ (Frequency/How often) _____

(Diagnosis/Symptoms/What is this being administered for?) _____

_____

3. (Medication) _____

(Dosage/How much) _____ (Frequency/How often) _____

(Diagnosis/Symptoms/What is this being administered for?) _____

_____

YES	NO	
_____	_____	My child may be given Tylenol.
_____	_____	My child may be given Benadryl.
_____	_____	My child may use insect repellent.
_____	_____	My child may use sunscreen.

Prescribed medication **must** be in a prescription bottle with a pharmacy label containing the child's name, the name of the medication, the dosage, and directions for administration. All nonprescription medication must be in the **original** container with directions for use, labeled with the child's name, and with a licensed prescriber's note.

Signed: _____ Relationship: _____ Date: _____

9

Take Nothing but Pictures, Leave Nothing but Footprints

If you concentrate on activities that are aimed at collecting data rather than specimens at field sites, you protect yourself as well as the environment. Before planning an activity that results in removing something from or irreversibly disturbing the field-study area, ask yourself if there is any reasonable way you could accomplish the same educational goals in another way. Science is more about observing than about collecting, so the less intervention with the observed system the better. If you and your students can observe without touching, so much the better. Let the hands be on the instruments rather than on the organisms. That way you minimize the hazards that unknown or unanticipated organisms can pose and you make the least number of changes in the ecosystem you visit. You minimize contacts with potential allergens or infectious agents and you avoid the inadvertent removal or harming of protected species.

On the other hand, plan on carrying out everything you bring into the field site including used materials, leftover supplies, and trash. Be aware that each outdoor environment has its own, perhaps unique, delicately balanced ecosystem. For that reason, you should not simply release classroom-raised organisms to the outdoors. They may be completely alien species, unable to survive or worse, with insufficient predators. The introduction of alien species can forever negatively alter an environment.

HELIUM BALLOONS AND NOTES IN BOTTLES

In the past, classes have prepared helium balloons and bottles with notes and return postcards. The helium balloons were released outdoors and the bottles were thrown out into the ocean with students eagerly awaiting returns that would tell them how far the balloons and bottles had traveled.

We now know that when the balloons finally disintegrate, the helium that is released can cause damage to the ozone layer of the upper atmosphere, and the containers cast into the sea can cause harm to sea creatures that might swallow them or otherwise come in contact with them. We strongly recommend you refrain from helium balloon and bottle note activities.

9

THE SAVVY SCIENCE TEACHER

Ms. Tallchief was completing a month-long electricity unit with her sixth graders when the students became fascinated with experiments they did on static electricity. The county science museum had several programs on electricity, so Ms. Tallchief contacted the educational program director at the museum to see if the museum had a program that could extend the static electricity activities that had been done in class.

Together, Ms. Tallchief and the museum staff modified two existing museum programs—one using the museum's large Van de Graaff generator and a weather program about lightning—to take advantage of the students' in-class activities and give them a safe experience in observing lightning-like strikes created by the Van de Graaff generator.

Working with the school librarian, Ms. Tallchief assigned trade books and magazine articles for students to read the week before the planned museum visit. Following the reading and research, the class prepared a list of questions that they would like answered during the museum visit. The class sent the questions by e-mail to the museum instructors and kept copies of the questions in notebooks they planned to bring to the museum.

9

Connections

▶ Adler, D.A., N. Tobin (Illustrator). 1999. *How Tall, How Short, How Faraway.* Holiday House.
▶ Foster, G.W. 1999. *Elementary Mathematics and Science Methods: Inquiry Teaching and Learning.* Arlington, Va.: NSTA Press.
▶ Keteyian, L. 2001. A Garden Story. *Science and Children* 39 (3): 22–25.
▶ Robertson, W.C. 2001. *Community Connections for Science Education: Building Successful Partnerships.* Arlington, Va.: NSTA Press.
▶ Russell, H.R. 2001. *Ten-Minute Field Trips.* Arlington, Va.: NSTA Press.

The Kitchen Sink

Ms. M. is seen entering school shortly after 7a.m. In her right hand is a tote bag full of papers, curriculum guides, several CD-ROMs with software she's been testing at home, the district policy bulletin on student Internet access, the latest newsletter from the county Discovery Museum, and the Red Cross manual for the CPR course she's been taking. There's also a clipboard with reminder notes: "Check photo permission slip; sign out video camera from the media center; ask school nurse about Tito's dust mite allergies; call Maria's guardian about eyeglasses." With her left hand she's balancing a box filled with soda straws, waxed paper, aluminum foil, and old newspapers that she's bringing in for the science activity center she'll set up this afternoon. On her wrist are a dozen rubber bands for students who come to class with shoulder-length hair—

Sometimes you wonder how you're going to get everything done. Each time you check off an item, two more appear. Those are the times to take stock of everything you've accomplished.

Science safety can be like that. Just when you think you have everything under control, a new concern emerges. Take heart. While our domain of concern grows broader each year, so do the supports for good teaching. Most of the topics in this chapter apply not just to safety in science activities but also to safe teaching practices in general.

Persistent Problems

Asthma, allergies, and other persistent symptoms seem to be on the rise as buildings are made more airtight. Be alert to such signs as lingering coughs, sneezing, eye rubbing, headaches, and lethargy.

The Not-So-Magic Carpet

Elementary classrooms have a great deal of carpet. This floor covering may be the source of a host of problems that may be difficult to trace or resolve. The glues and adhesives from newly installed carpet may out-gas, causing mild but persistent headaches or dizziness. Infrequently or improperly cleaned carpets can harbor dust mites, mold, and other allergens and disease-causing organisms. Spilled fluids can

10

penetrate to carpet backing and padding, so surfaces that appear clean may be covering contaminated material below. The upholstery of old furniture may pose problems similar to carpets.

If you suspect that your classroom carpets are causing student problems, request a thorough cleaning with mildew treatment. Make sure that the classroom is ventilated after treatment so that it dries quickly. Unfortunately, some dander cannot be removed from carpets so it is important to avoid having guinea pigs and rabbits on them.

The Class Menagerie

If you have animals or many plants in your room, the food, waste, and soils can harbor mold and spores that last for years in the air of a classroom. Parasitic cysts from human waste, classroom pets, and dissection specimens can resist all common cleaning agents. Limit your plants and use commercial potting soil. Never bring dead animals of any kind into the classroom. (See Chapter 5, **Lively Science.**)

Combustible Fabrics

Ask for help from your local fire department to demonstrate the high combustibility of fabrics, especially the filmy, gauzy fabrics that are popular in contemporary clothing.

Teach children what to do if clothing catches fire. Have kids demonstrate drop-and-roll to parents and siblings.

Piercings pose another problem for the science classroom. No jewelry should hang or protrude from a working scientist. If a student insists that a particular piece of jewelry cannot be removed, cover it completely with a bandage.

Heavy Metal Is Not Just Loud Music

Heavy metal and organic compounds can persist in cracks and crevices in flooring and furniture despite regular cleaning. Many such compounds that were frequently used for science activities and cleaning in years past are now known to be hazardous—toxic or carcinogenic. If you occupy an older facility, particularly one that may have been used for upper-grade science programs, make sure that such things as mercury from broken thermometers are not still around.

Dress of the Day

Today's school uniform? Earrings, tank tops, wide-legged or low-slung slacks, fluffy, gauzy fabrics, and whatever today's MTV stars are wearing. Unfortunately, many clothing fashions make poor choices for science activities.

Begin with the philosophy that the classroom is a "workplace"—an environment where commonsense clothing is required. Loose, floppy clothing and hanging jewelry are not reasonable. Coats, jackets, hats, and similar loose-fitting, overhanging, and dangling articles should be removed and stored away from work and lab areas. Absorbent watch-

10

bands and wrist ornaments should be removed. Hair should be tied, pinned, or otherwise secured back behind the shoulders. Backpacks and totes should be stored in cubbies. Shoes should have closed toes and be securely tied. No platform shoes or any other footwear that is likely to result in tripping and falling should be worn. This is a matter of safe practice rather than fashion commentary. And of course, remind the adults (especially aides, interns, and student teachers) to dress likewise.

Eye Wear

Contact lenses, especially soft contact lenses, can absorb chemical fumes or otherwise trap chemicals in the eye, rendering eyewash ineffective. The standard rule is "contacts out, glasses on" when participating in any activity that would require safety glasses. If some students say they don't have regular glasses, you should confer directly with the parents or guardians to explain the hazard of contact lens use during science activities and see if you can find a mutually acceptable resolution.

Many teachers associate eye protection with chemistry activities, but it's a must in many other circumstances. Any activity that can generate projectiles requires eye protection. That includes dissection because the preservatives and parts can splash, squirt, or otherwise become airborne. Make sure the safety goggles are certified for safety and are not just the "plant visitor specs." (See Chapter 6, **Modern Alchemy.**) If safety goggles are shared, they must be sterilized after every use, either in a UV cabinet or in hot water and detergent or disinfectant, to prevent the spread of conjunctivitis and hepatitis. It is always better to prevent eye accidents with goggles—but if an accident happens, have the eyewash clean and ready. (See Chapter 3, **Where Science Happens.**)

The Internet Connection

The National Science Education Standards encourage teachers to go beyond the walls of their classrooms, taking their students both virtually and physically into contact with real science. If you have Internet access, there are many wonderful science activities and assignments that you should be encouraging. But you should also remember that you are responsible for ensuring that your students' work on the Internet is carefully designed and supervised so they are safe as they venture into this complex learning environment.

If your district has developed an Internet-use policy and a written contract to be signed by students and parents, be sure you know the policy and follow it carefully. Remember that, unlike formal print publications, the information posted on Internet websites need not be edited or vetted. False, misleading, and downright dangerous information is just as prevalent on the Internet as accurate, up-to-date, and useful information. It is therefore essential that you provide students with Internet

10

assignments that are carefully structured and that you have screened sites you intend them to use.

Unsupervised exploration is an invitation to disaster. While most schools today have Internet filters in place, it is important to remember that they are not foolproof. Many sites offer potentially dangerous information—not only pornographers, but hate groups, anarchists, and members of cults and fringe groups use the Net to contact young people. The Net filters do not screen for all of these potential dangers.

Make sure that your students have clear, timely assignments and that their use of the Net is always supervised. That may mean arranging the monitors so that they can be seen by an adult supervisor at all times, or you may need to circulate around the room to view all the screens.

Under no circumstances should students be allowed to provide their full names or demographic information on the Net. E-mails to student pen pals should be screened through the teacher, using first names or pseudonyms. If you share group pictures of experiments or discoveries on the Net, identify by class, not by individual names.

SAMPLE INTERNET-USE GUIDELINES AND CONTRACT

Source: *The Brookline Public Schools, Mass.*

GUIDELINES

The primary purpose of the Internet connection is educational; therefore, the_____ School(s)

▷ *Takes no responsibility for any information or materials that are transferred through the Internet and requires users to refrain from downloading inappropriate, non-educational material;*

▷ *Will not be liable for the actions of anyone connecting to the Internet through this hook-up. All users shall assume full liability, legal, financial, or otherwise, for their actions;*

▷ *Makes no guarantees, implied or otherwise, regarding the reliability of the data connection. The _____ Schools shall not be liable for any loss or corruption of data resulting from use of the Internet connection;*

▷ *Reserves the right to examine all data stored in computers or on disks which are the property of the _____ Schools to ensure that users are in compliance with these regulations;*

10

- *Strongly condemns the illegal acquisition and/or distribution of software, otherwise known as pirating. Any users transferring such files through the Internet, and any whose accounts are found to contain such illegal files, may have their accounts permanently revoked;*

- *Reminds all users that when they use the Internet, they are entering a global community, and any actions taken by them will reflect upon the school system as a whole. As such, we expect that all users will behave in an ethical and legal manner;*

- *Reserves the right to change or modify these rules at any time without notice.*

CONTRACT

I, _____, agree:

To abide by all rules which are listed in the _____ Schools Guidelines for Internet Use;

That the primary purpose of the _____ Schools Internet connection is educational;

That the use of the Internet is a privilege, not a right;

Not to participate in the transfer of inappropriate or illegal materials, including the intellectual property of others through the _____ Schools Internet connection;

Not to allow other individuals to use my account for Internet activities, nor will I give anyone my password.

I understand that inappropriate behavior may lead to penalties, which may include discipline, revocation of account, or legal action.

I realize that there are inappropriate and possibly offensive materials available to those who use the Internet, and the undersigned hereby releases the _____ Schools from any liability or damages that may result from the viewing of, or contact with, such materials.

Signed:_____ Date:_____

Parents must sign if the user is under eighteen years of age.

I, _____, the parent/guardian of the above, agree to accept all financial and legal liabilities which may result from my son's/daughter's use of the _____ Schools Internet connection.

Signed:_____ Date:_____

10

MY INTERNET CONTRACT

I, _____, promise to obey all school policies and rules about the Internet. I will only use search engines for appropriate school assignments. I will avoid inappropriate sites. I will not join chat rooms or use a personal e-mail account at school. I will not download material or change the settings on school computers. I understand that violation of these rules may result in discipline and loss of all computer privileges.

_____(Student)   _____(Parents)

You probably won't need a permission slip for—

▶ The football team scoring the winning touchdown
▶ The finale of the school Christmas play
▶ A long shot of a crowded hallway for a bond issue brochure
▶ A "mood shot" of students getting off a bus on the first day of school

You should get parental permission to photograph—

▶ Two students doing an experiment
▶ A student getting special assistance
▶ Media or police interviews

Picture This

Even public schools are private places from the standpoint of student protection. While students are under our care, we must maintain their privacy and uphold their rights. One area that often becomes an issue is the photographing of students.

At the beginning of each year, make sure that district-approved parental consent documents have been obtained and filed before any photographs are taken. Before releasing any photographs to an outside entity, make sure that you have the clear written consent of the parent or guardian and that you are following district rules.

Special circumstances may make even standard photo releases inappropriate. Students are sometimes the subjects of custody disputes, and photos can endanger their safety. Photos of disabled students and students in special needs classrooms might inadvertently subject a child to possible public ridicule. Photos of students in certain disciplinary or instructional situations might imply some negative connotations. When in doubt, ask the parents again.

Your students and their parents have a reasonable expectation of privacy while they are in your care and they rely on your judgment. Reporters,

10

researchers, and even police agency representatives do not have the right to question students without parental consent. One major exception—in almost every state, representatives of agencies responsible for child protective services and prevention of child abuse may question students in the presence of a school official without the permission of their parents.

Many schools allow students to produce videos for cable channels. When a regular student news or weather program is produced, you may be able to provide parents with a blanket permission slip for participation. If a special topic is planned, parents should again be asked for consent. This includes assignments where students are creating videos for science projects.

At the Beginning of Every Year

- Obtain photo releases for every student.
- Check the records of each student to see if any special privacy procedures apply.
- Review all Individualized Education Programs (IEPs) for requirements and accommodations for your students.
- Check medical records for allergies and other precautions.

SAMPLE CONSENT AND RELEASE FORM

Source: *The Brookline Public Schools, Mass.*

Dear Parents:

We are often approached by reporters from newspapers, magazines, and television to interview, photograph, and/or videotape our students. These members of the press are often motivated to make these requests because of the nature of our instructional programs. Occasionally they will simply want a picture of children coming to school on the opening day. In addition, we may have textbook companies request that they be able to photograph a classroom at work to include in a recent publication.

We do not allow any children to be interviewed/photographed, and/or videotaped by the media and/or school personnel for publicity or news papers without having your permission. I am asking that you indicate below whether you are willing to grant such permission. Please complete the tear-off and return it to your child's classroom teacher. Thank you for your assistance.

(Signature) _____

10

The Scientific Gourmet

Investigations with food and cooking have long been a part of science activities. However, these investigations present special problems that should be taken into account in planning activities.

Cook and Eat Elsewhere

There are many suggestions for edible science activities in books and curriculum resources. But there should be no eating in a science facility. The hidden dangers that come with consumption of food or drink in a science room or science activity area fall into two categories. First, the area can be contaminated with surprisingly persistent toxins, including heavy metals, organic compounds, molds, and pathogens. Second, students who are in the habit of eating in a science workspace may be tempted to taste a material that is meant for research. In a shared science space, you can never be sure of what materials were there before or how well the space was cleaned. In self-contained classrooms, teachers can sometimes prepare a specific cooking/eating space, but in general, this should never be the same place the students use for science activities. The best rule is the most simple: Nothing should be tasted or eaten as part of science lab work.

But what about those motivating experiences that involve foods, such as observing changes in churning cream to butter or gathering and roasting pumpkin seeds? The best strategy is to move the activity to a different locale—one associated with food preparation and not with science activities—the cafeteria or home economics room.

Nut Allergies

An increasing number of students and adults have been identified with serious (often life-threatening) allergies to nuts. An allergic reaction may be triggered not only by ingestion but also by proximity to a nut or nut product. If such an allergic individual is present in your class, then investigations involving nuts, nut oils, and nut by-

10

products must be avoided. School authorities may also have to take steps to eliminate these products in breakfast and lunch programs and provide separated eating facilities to ensure that there is no exposure from snacks or other foods brought into the classroom or school building.

The Latex Connection

Balloons have been a common item in elementary classrooms. The most commonly used latex balloon can present a dual hazard—a choking hazard for young children and an allergy hazard for adults and children. Do not allow young children to try and blow up balloons or work unsupervised with uninflated balloons. In addition, latex has been found to be a serious allergen—causing reactions as simple as rash and irritation and as serious as anaphylactic shock.

First Aid and Standard Precautions (formerly known as "Universal Precautions")

It's reasonable and prudent to be prepared for the unexpected. First aid training courses from the American Red Cross are highly recommended. Most states have Good Samaritan laws that provide liability protection. Check to find the specifics in your state.

An EpiPen or Adrenalin injection is a prescribed instrument that can be of critical importance to severely allergic people. Without it, anaphylactic shock from an insect sting could result in a fatality. Although relatively simple to use, it must be administered by a nurse or person trained by the prescribing physician. Find out about your district policy, and make sure you or someone else is trained to use an EpiPen.

The handling of body fluids such as blood, saliva, and vomitus requires prior training in the proper procedures to protect against transmission of blood-borne pathogens such as HIV or hepatitis. The accepted standard of care is to use Standard Precautions in all instances involving body fluids. Check with your school health officer for specifics on how the OSHA Blood-Borne Pathogen Standards are implemented in your district. All persons should be treated as if they might be infectious—no exceptions.

Standard Precautions

▶ Always have gloves handy for use with bleeding students.
▶ Never interfere in a fight, which might involve blood or biting.
▶ Never bring blood or blood products into the classroom.
▶ All designated personnel who might be asked to clean up blood, saliva, or vomitus should be vaccinated for hepatitis.
▶ Use proven disinfectant for blood or body fluid spills.
▶ Designate a special disposal area for blood and saliva, medical products, and sharps.

Refer to your school and community health services for more specifics.

10

E.T. Phone Home—or Send E-Mail

Teachers need telephones and e-mail in their classrooms for ordinary communications as well as for emergencies. Parents need to be partners in your work with their children, and communication is critical to this partnership. The better teachers and parents know each other, the better they can work together to support kids and ensure their safety at home and at school. At the very least, you need a functioning means of calling for help or to report a problem instantly. Keep a log of your calls and other communications to document your ongoing efforts to keep everyone properly informed.

Crisis Response Team

It is highly recommended that school systems and individual schools create and train crisis response teams to respond to medical and psychological crises, threats and acts of violence, and the range of circumstances that require immediate action for the welfare and safety of students and others in the schools. Such teams should proactively plan for emergencies that could arise and ensure that appropriate individuals are trained and available to provide first aid, psychological support, physical security, and public information. Such teams should include and/or maintain regular contact with representatives from state and local agencies that provide assistance and emergency response (e.g., police and fire departments, community mental-health agencies, local hospitals, state health department).

Planning for the Future

It may be years before your facilities are due for major renovation or a brand-new building, but before that happens, there are improvements you can request to make your science teaching safer and more effective next year. When your principal begins to discuss next year's assignments, consider these priorities:

- *Class size:* While additional facilities and equipment can make science safer for larger groups of students, there's a limit to the number of students that can be effectively and safely taught an active investigative science program. There is a very high, positive correlation between class size and accident rate, no matter how good the facilities. While experts disagree on an absolute limit, statistics show that accidents increase dramatically as classes increase beyond 20–24 students.

- *Scheduling:* Preparation for science activities takes thought and time. Equipment needs to be inventoried and checked for correct and safe functioning. Surfaces need to be cleaned before and after messy activities. This kind of preparation cannot be done during a five-minute break or while students are doing seatwork. Preparation time needs to be scheduled rather than squeezed in,

10

especially if you are team teaching, need to share space, or need to move from one location to another.

▶ **Security:** If there is a choice, request a room with two exit doors, but not one in a heavy-traffic area or near a major school entrance. Check for heating and ventilation and for good communication with the office. Get a phone and make sure it's on. If you suspect there are old copies of your classroom key floating around, ask for your room to be rekeyed. Keys to science storage areas and rooms solely dedicated to science instruction should be unique. These rooms should not be accessible with keys used to enter regular classrooms or common areas.

THE SAVVY SCIENCE TEACHER

Dara D. capitalizes on her students' spring fever in order to review their study of photosynthesis. Each February the students watch for the first signs of leaves on the local maple trees: new leaves mean transpiration will resume. They collect sap from the maple trees in the schoolyard in clean metal buckets that are only used for that purpose. She uses Crockpots to boil the syrup down in the teacher's lounge.

In return for their help in watching her pots boil, Dara invites the faculty to a pancake breakfast staged in the school cafeteria. The room is decorated with posters on how plants make sugar and how proteins (egg albumin) change when heated. Students are quick to serve science along with breakfast—and they can explain why they never eat in their science lab. This delicious lesson is both safe and scientific.

Connections

▶ American Chemical Society. 2001. *Chemical Safety for Teachers and Their Supervisors.* Washington, D.C.: American Chemical Society.

▶ *www.safeschoolsamerica. com/StandardsList.htm*

▶ *www.ibiblio.org/nppa/ sherer/sherer12.html*

10

Live Long
and Prosper

Consider the changes. Yesterday's one-room schoolhouse had one teacher responsible for every subject, every grade, and maintenance of the classroom and schoolhouse. Today's self-contained classroom has one teacher responsible for a diverse group of students with widely ranging abilities and needs; integrated learning of subjects from the basics to social and behavioral issues; and a roomful of widgets—high-tech, low-tech, and all that's in between. Everything has changed, yet everything remains the same. You, the teacher, remain responsible for everyone and for everything that goes on in your classroom—both an awesome responsibility and a world of opportunity.

Four Ps for Professionals

You are the professional. Your responsibilities include more than just the education of your students. You also act *in loco parentis*—in a legal sense, in place of parents for the children assigned to you. You can assume these responsibilities because you

> **PREPARE:** Your formal education and studies leading to qualification and certification to teach are just the beginning of your professional training and development. You constantly keep up to date with continuing education by joining and actively participating in professional organizations and by reading journals and research reports in education, instructional strategies, and subject areas. You make yourself thoroughly familiar with the learning expectations and standards set by federal, state, and local authorities and take the time to analyze and compare these to other sources of information—recommendations of professional organizations, research data, and your own knowledge and training. You make sure that you read and understand all school policies and procedures that relate to your duties and responsibilities—reviewing and filing new information and bulletins that update manuals and other official documents.

11

▶ **PLAN:** You take the time to consider what you are required to teach and the best strategies to employ so as to ensure your students can learn effectively and safely. You write out your plans, not just so others can read them, but so you can review and critique them yourself before you begin and after the lesson is over. If you have interns, student teachers, aides, parent volunteers, or any other assistants, you determine how best to train them to work effectively and safely with you and your students. You think ahead about the learning styles, maturity, and behavior of each of your students and determine how best to work with their strengths and their limitations.

▶ **PREVENT:** You take the time to assess hazards and review procedures for accident prevention. You teach and review safety procedures with every student and adult every time a hazard is anticipated. You post safety signs and keep copies of safety information. If you detect safety hazards that you cannot mitigate, you put your concerns and requests for assistance or changes in writing to the appropriate supervisor and do not use the defective equipment until the hazard is mitigated.

▶ **PROTECT:** You check your facilities for the presence and accessibility of correctly specified and correctly operating safety equipment and protective devices. You count the number of protective devices that you have, such as safety glasses or aprons, to ensure that you have enough for everyone who needs them. You demonstrate and instruct students and helpers on the proper use of safety equipment and protective gear. You keep records of safety lessons and instructions to ensure that no one has missed getting the information. You insist on the use of protective devices by everyone in the room, including yourself and all visitors.

Broadening Your Definition of Safety

As classroom teacher and science teacher, you need to consider safety as broadly as possible. The prior chapters of this book are not intended to be an exhaustive manual of everything you must do or know to ensure safe science investigations. Rather, they are meant to sharpen your observational skills so that you recognize the issues and circumstances that require your attention and planning in order for you to conduct science inquiry safely. No single book or series of books can anticipate all the safety issues that can arise in an active science program. Nor can any book, this one included, anticipate what new information and technology will render the advice given inaccurate or incorrect. It is the habit of observing and thinking about science lessons with common sense and safety in mind that will keep you and your students safe.

A Diversity of Needs

Your students probably are quite diverse in their needs, their abilities, and their prior experiences. These issues must be taken into account in your planning and your activities. Remember that accommodation and modification are your legal and professional

11

responsibilities. You cannot delegate that to the special education department, nor can the special education department leave you to your own devices. Have you prepared for special physical needs, special educational needs, and special behavioral needs? It is your responsibility to read Individualized Education Programs (IEPs) and to be prepared to meet the requirements defined in them. Your special education personnel are obligated to help explain IEP goals and objectives to you on request. Other students may have needs identified under Section 504 of the Americans with Disabilities Act. Even though they are not special education students, they are entitled to modifications and these are a general education legal responsibility.

"Look at Me—Talk to Me"

Science safety encompasses more than technique and equipment. Science activities are usually designed for students to work more freely and cooperatively in an interactive setting. Students often work in pairs or small groups and are encouraged to discuss observations and plan together. You have the opportunity to observe students' behavioral characteristics in an informal setting. How well do they work in groups? Are leadership qualities emerging? Are some of your quieter students finally becoming animated and engaged? On the other hand, is someone exceptionally quiet or sad or unable to handle anger effectively? Do you have students who are always left out or picked on? Use these observational opportunities to get a better picture of the individuals in your class. As a first-line observer, you are often in the best position to know if a student needs help of a nonacademic nature. Reach out, talk, and share your observations with parents and with professionals who may provide additional assistance.

Volunteer Help

Many hands make light work and often, better science education. But adult volunteers can be a mixed blessing in a busy classroom. If you have regular or occasional helpers and volunteers, you bear the ultimate responsibility for their actions, so make sure you have planned sufficient time to train and instruct them. Many municipalities also require security and criminal background checks on all persons who will come in contact with students. Make sure you know the rules and follow them strictly.

Substitute Teachers, Interns, and Student Teachers

The actions of substitute teachers, interns, and student teachers in your classroom are also part of your responsibility. They are considered to be implementing your plans, your rules, and your instructions. Unless you are certain that these persons are able and qualified to properly and safely conduct an activity, do not plan for active investigation to be carried out when you are not present. Keep a separate set of lesson plans that may be substituted for science lab activities if you should be absent unexpectedly.

11

Guests and Others

You also need to safeguard yourself and your students from well-meaning or not-so-well-meaning guests or intruders. Investigative science activities usually generate more excitement and more physical movement than most other activities, so it's best to avoid adding guests to these activities.

In some schools, surprise guests and observers are commonplace. If this is the case for you, be sure that all such persons are first cleared by the school administration. This is particularly important if your class includes a student involved in a dispute about custody or guardianship.

If visitors attend a class when all or some students are engaged in science activities, make sure that they are first made aware of all safety rules and practices. You may even want to use the visit as an opportunity to have your students review the rules: Stop briefly and ask your students to explain the rules to the visitor.

You need to be aware of anyone who enters your classroom. Keep doors that open directly to the outside locked from the inside and make sure that your students know that they should not open the door except with your permission.

GUESTS IN YOUR CLASSROOM

You are responsible for the conduct of everyone who enters your classroom—students as well as assistants and visitors.

▷ Be sure you are aware of everyone who enters, who they are, and whether they have a legitimate reason for being there.

▷ If you have a classroom door that opens directly to the outside, make sure that it can only be opened from the inside and that students understand that only an adult may open it.

▷ During science lab activities that involve special techniques or safety precautions, admit only those who have been adequately instructed and who are prepared to follow safe procedures. This includes supervisors and other observers. They should understand that they should come for the entire sequence of instruction or return at another time.

▷ Screen and prepare all anticipated guests. For adult visitors, including volunteers, you need to make sure that all required security and criminal offender records index (CORI) checks have been made prior to the visit. You may need to explain the process and gain permission.

> If you are planning to have guest speakers, make sure you have taken the time to thoroughly plan for their presentations and that all safety issues have been addressed.

Legal Responsibilities

You cannot prevent a lawsuit from being filed. No matter how unjust or frivolous, our legal system provides the opportunity for people to take their complaints to court. There are, however, many things that you can do to prevent being found at fault or liable.

The Jargon

If an accident occurs, people like to try and fix blame. It is common practice to sue everyone with any connection to the event just to find out which charge can be made to stick. Malpractice attorneys litigate matters of professional misfeasance, nonfeasance, and malfeasance. Here are some simplified definitions:

> **Misfeasance:** Performance of a lawful action in an illegal or improper manner. In a science activity, this might result from using an incorrect chemical for an experiment or too much of the correct chemical. It might include selecting an activity that is inappropriate for the students to whom it was assigned. The further you deviate from the recommended district curriculum, the greater the risk you take on for yourself.

> **Nonfeasance:** Omission or failure to do what ought to be done. This could include failure to provide eye protection or fire equipment, or to post a standard fire drill exit procedure. If you have eye protection available but did not make sure your students were using the protection when needed, this could also be considered an omission with liability. Being out of your room when your students are in class can create a nonfeasance liability. If students you are responsible for are working in an alcove, a hall, or some part of the room where you cannot see and supervise them, you could have a nonfeasance problem.

> **Malfeasance:** Intentional wrongdoing, deliberate violation of law or standard, or mismanagement of responsibilities. Ignorance is no excuse. If there is a governing law or regulation or local written policy, you are responsible for knowing about it and conforming. Many states have benchmarks or standards that include safety precautions and lessons. These can have the effect of law even though there is no penalty statute. For example, an adopted state standard may require that you teach some safety procedure but doesn't specify a penalty if you do not. In the event of an accident that might have been prevented with the safety procedure, your failure to teach the procedure may not result in a criminal charge against you but it could be construed as malfeasance for which you can be found liable.

11

- District policy manuals and all subsequent policy communications
- State and local curriculum guides
- Lesson plan book
- Attendance and grade book—with correlations to the lesson plan book and records of safety lessons for each individual student
- Inventory of materials and equipment
- Maintenance requests
- Purchase requisitions
- Records and notes of professional development activities

A *tort* is a wrong that you do to someone. If you give students the wrong instructions or fail to provide appropriate safe instructions for performing an activity and the activity results in accident or injury, your action is a tort.

The Best Defense

Sounds intimidating? Perhaps, but you can reduce your exposure to these liabilities dramatically by making safe practice a habit. Here are some tips:

- Document your preparation for safety. Subscribe to journals, read books, and take classes to keep up to date.

- As part of your lesson plans and records, document safety lessons and make sure you keep records of follow-up with safety lessons for children who are absent.

- Do not leave the premises when you are responsible for students. And do not permit students to work where they are out of your sight and supervision.

- Put your safety needs in writing. Don't just complain: Explain why equipment and maintenance needs are necessary. Follow up on your requests. Don't stop until the situation is corrected. Do not engage in any activity involving a reported safety hazard until the hazard is mitigated.

- In case you are involved in potential litigation, make sure you have the advice, and possibly the presence, of an attorney who represents your interests before making any statements to anyone else.

Insurance

Lawsuits are expensive, even if they are dismissed or you are found not to be responsible. You probably have some insurance that covers you for basic liability. But it can cost tens of thousands of dollars just to get a nuisance suit in front of a judge so that you can have it dismissed. Before that time, there will be accusations, investigations, and depositions. That's why insurance is vital.

Begin by investigating what coverage you already have. Most school systems have errors and omissions (E & O) coverage for the institution and its employees. This will cover mistakes. But it may have exclusions. Find out what the exceptions are. Insurance policies generally exclude any action that violates the law, and that can be the "Catch-22." If the law says you must teach the fire drill procedure or prohibits the use of alcohol burners, you may find yourself without insurance coverage if you violate the law. Most district policies cover employees but they may not cover volunteers or visitors. Check.

You may have liability insurance through your union or professional association. In general, these policies will cover the preliminary costs of a lawsuit. They will get you a lawyer quickly, separate from the one that represents the district, and get you preliminary advice. But many of these policies exclude any punitive damages, so the cost of your lawyer may be covered but not the biggest part of a future settlement.

Many teachers carry extra professional coverage through their homeowner's or renter's policy. You can obtain an umbrella policy to extend coverage and back up other liability policies that you may have. This might also be a rider for professional liability on an existing policy, usually at very little additional cost. This kind of coverage is highly recommended.

Take Heart

With all this talk of litigation and liability you may be asking, "Is inquiry worth it?" With absolute confidence we say, "Yes." When you take the time to prepare to safely conduct an active investigative science program, you not only assist your students in answering the questions on their next test, you prepare your students to answer future questions we have yet to imagine. Your habit of conducting work thoughtfully and safely becomes the model for the conduct of your students at home and in their future endeavors. As first teacher in space, Christa McAuliffe, so elegantly put it, we touch the future when we teach.

11

THE SAVVY SCIENCE TEACHER

Jeff N. loves to create problems for students. Sometimes they even create their own and then design careful procedures to discover the answers. There are no cookbook directions in Jeff's labs, and his students love it. But they would not have been able to work that way six months ago.

While other members of his department were abandoning labs because of discipline problems, Jeff was encouraging students to design their own. To teach his students organization and self-discipline, Jeff introduced one component of a lab at a time.

First, scientific questioning; then "If...then" hypotheses. Each lab technique was taught separately with plenty of chances to practice and an emphasis on safety. Finally, Jeff challenged his students to develop procedures through which their questions could be investigated *safely.* Student peer groups critiqued the procedures for safety concerns, and when both teacher and student peers gave the procedures "S" grades, the students were ready to begin. Taking responsibility one step at a time, Jeff N.'s students are well on their way to becoming scientists.

11

Conclusion

Teaching is an incredibly complex process. You make dozens of instructional decisions each hour. You manage an environment, a curriculum, and a community of learners. Sometimes the details can become so daunting that you must allocate time to refocus.

Safety issues are that way, too. This book has presented eleven chapters of ideas, warnings, and potential hazards. To connect these ideas to reality, we have included anecdotes—some almost verbatim and some composites—of actual experiences of teachers and supervisors. They are meant to illustrate both the risks and the opportunities in the familiar environment of your classroom.

If these ideas have sharpened your perceptions or raised your antennae, all the better. But if they've dampened your enthusiasm for exploration, look again. The principles of each chapter are positive, constructive, and practical. Here's your review:

1 Setting the Scene

- Introduce exploration slowly, one skill at a time, gradually increasing the time on task.
- Model the behaviors of professional scientists as you teach responsibility and organization.
- Make students become partners in safety procedures so that safe work habits become second nature.
- Bring parents and other school staff onto your safety team to support your lessons.
- Integrate science safety with other subjects by writing, drawing, and communicating the big ideas.

2 Communities of Learners

- Plan science activities that are accessible to all students.
- Eliminate barriers in your room by removing clutter and freeing up space.
- Communicate your needs for support in modifying your program for special needs students.
- Minimize the potential for disruptive behavior with shorter and more specific tasks.
- Investigate adaptive equipment and technologies with consultants and district support staff.

3 Where Science Happens

▷ Conduct science activities in facilities that provide adequate space and ventilation for safety.

▷ Provide hot and cold running water in science activity areas.

▷ Select furniture that is stable but easily rearranged, and provide unobstructed flat work surfaces.

▷ Ensure that safety equipment such as fire extinguishers and eyewashes are operational and accessible.

▷ Make sure that electrical service and wiring to your room are well-maintained, provide adequate amperage, and include appropriate ground fault circuit interrupter protection.

4 Finders Keepers

▷ Provide ample open storage to encourage students to obtain and return simple science supplies easily and safely.

▷ Include enough locked storage, inaccessible to students, for valuable and fragile supplies and equipment as well as materials too hazardous for direct student access.

▷ Use locked cabinets specifically appropriate for storage of chemicals.

▷ Keep incompatible chemicals separated—arrange storage by chemical properties, not by alphabetical order.

▷ Make sure chemical inventories are accurate, updated, and regularly reviewed.

▷ Maintain Materials Safety Data Sheets (MSDS) for every product—one set in the office and one set in your classroom.

▷ Prepare materials and supplies for science activities in an adequate, ventilated, and well-lit preparation space away from students and other traffic.

▷ Clear out excess supplies, equipment, and furniture regularly as a vital part of safe practice.

5 Lively Science

▷ Maintain living cultures to provide students with opportunities for important lessons in safety and care.

▷ Choose organisms that are appropriate for the space and time you have to devote to them and the behavior and maturity of your students. Never opt for headlines over good science.

- Begin with simple organisms—plants and invertebrates—before trying to maintain more complex and difficult ones.
- Never bring wild or feral animals into the classroom.
- Avoid organisms that are toxic or highly allergenic.
- Inform students and parents of your cultures and be aware of unusual allergies.

6 Modern Alchemy

- Emphasize careful process skills over drama.
- Build responsibility gradually.
- Use microscale experiments for safety and to encourage careful observation.
- Choose less toxic and dangerous options over traditional labs now known to be hazardous.
- Maintain a minimal quantity and variety of chemicals—less is better.
- Require the use of appropriate safety equipment by all persons—children and adults—at all times.

7 Striking Gold

- Rocks and minerals are hard, sharp, and heavy. Teach students safe procedures for moving heavy objects and using tools before beginning activities.
- Never allow the tasting of specimens.
- Keep students away from contaminated soils and insist on proper hand-washing.
- Never permit direct observation of the Sun.
- Review rules and procedures prior to field studies.

8 Falling for Science

- Become familiar with and follow the guidelines for use of all school equipment.
- Use light and sound experiments to teach students how to prevent damage to eyes and ears.
- Make sure all electrical connections are safe and conform to code.
- Teach and use the "one-hand rule" when working with electric circuits.
- Plan ahead so your room won't have physical barriers such as loose cords and other tripping and falling hazards.

9 The Great Outdoors

▷ Link field trips and field studies to curriculum goals.

▷ Preview the site and abutting properties before planning your field study.

▷ Determine proper clothing and footwear for the site and activities planned.

▷ Meet with cooperating resource people to plan activities.

▷ Orient and train all chaperones in your planned activities and in safety precautions.

10 The Kitchen Sink

▷ Minimize the use of carpets and upholstered furniture to reduce the growth and harboring of dust mites, mold spores, and other allergens.

▷ Regularly and carefully clean living cultures in the room.

▷ Check for the presence of heavy-metal contamination from prior activities— remove and appropriately dispose of all mercury and mercury-based instruments.

▷ Review appropriate clothing, covering, and eyewear for laboratory work.

▷ Ensure proper supervision in using the Internet.

▷ Obtain proper consent forms before photographing students.

▷ Do not prepare food or eat in science activity areas.

▷ Prepare with first aid training, crisis response training, and regular communication with parents.

▷ Plan with others for small class sizes, appropriate scheduling, and adequate and appropriate space and materials for an active science program.

▷ Make safety and security a significant concern of everyone.

11 Live Long and Prosper

▷ Prepare, plan, prevent, and protect.

▷ Become familiar with your school policies and with federal, state, and local laws.

▷ Document everything you do.

▷ Assess your safety lessons and keep good records.

▷ Take responsibility to supervise and train your assistants and volunteers.

▷ Make sure you are adequately protected with liability insurance.

Appendix A

Chemicals to Go—Candidates for Disposal

The chemicals in the following table may be found in science labs and classrooms because they were frequently used in older programs and demonstrations. They now are generally considered too hazardous to store and use in pre-college programs. You should check the materials you have in your classroom and stockroom. Anything you do not need for your current program should be removed. If your current program requires any of the chemicals in this table, you should review the hazards involved and consider replacing with a safer alternative.

If you find these or other hazardous materials, **do not just discard or dump these items.** Most require special handling and special disposal. Some may have decomposed to the extent that even moving or opening the stock bottles may present a serious toxicity or explosion hazard. Consult with professional hazardous waste experts such as those with your state environmental protection agencies.

The Merck Index, published and updated regularly by Merck & Co., Inc. is an excellent reference for determining the hazards of chemicals, as is the Flinn Chemical Catalog.

Chemical Name	Chemical Formula	Possible Appearance	Outdated Use	Hazard— Comments
White phosphorous	P	White or yellowish waxy-looking sticks stored in water	Demonstrate spontaneous combustion	Spontaneous combustion— fire that is very difficult to extinguish; small particles remaining continue to reignite
Elemental sodium	Na	Grayish non-uniform lumps	Explosive oxidation	Explosion with release of concentrated NaOH fumes and spray
Elemental mercury	Hg	Silver-colored liquid	Thermometers and barometers; illustration of density; electromotive replacement demos	Highly toxic; absorbed through the skin; vapors readily absorbed via respiratory tract
Chloroform	$CHCl_3$	Clear, colorless liquid	Anesthetic	Human inhalation can cause death; EPA lists as carcinogen
Potassium cyanide	KCN	White granules or powder	Insect killing jars	Violent poison; decomposes on exposure to air and moisture to produce deadly cyanide gas
Carbon tetrachloride	CCl_4	Clear, colorless liquid	Organic solvent	Poison by inhalation and skin absorption; carcinogen
Formaldehyde		Colorless clear or cloudy liquid	Preservative	Skin and mucous membrane irritant
Chlordane		Amber-colored liquid	Pesticide	Easily absorbed through skin and mucous membranes; highly toxic; EPA has banned from use
Silver cyanide	AgCN	White or grayish powder	Silver plating; creating mirrored surfaces	Highly toxic

Chemical Name	Chemical Formula	Possible Appearance	Outdated Use	Hazard— Comments
Potassium chlorate	$KClO_3$	White crystals	Generation of oxygen	Highly unstable, explosive
Calcium carbide	CaC_2	Grayish-black lumps	Mixed with water to release acetylene	Fire and explosion hazard
Benedict's solution		Blue liquid	Test for sugar	Caustic—not appropriate below high school level
Concentrated inorganic acids	(e.g., HNO_3, HCl, H_2SO_4)	Liquids	Various	Highly corrosive; some are volatile as well; serious burn and eye damage hazard. Purchase in smallest quantities possible; purchase pre-diluted solutions when ever possible. When diluting, always add acid to water and NEVER water to acid; beware of exothermic reaction and splash hazard
Picric acid	2,4,6-trinitro-phenol	Clear to yellowish liquid	Specimen preservative	Decomposes over time to become unstable explosive
Ammonium dichromate	$(NH_4)_2 Cr_2O_7$	Red-orange crystals	Demonstration volcanoes	Unstable; produces toxic by-products when burned
Magnesium strips	Mg	Slim silvery coiled metal	Wicks for demo volcanoes; "sparklers"	Burns at very high temperature releasing light that may damage eyes
Diethyl ether	$C_2H_5OC_2H_5$	Clear liquid in a can	Anesthetizing insects	Explosive

Appendix B

American Chemical Society Safety Guidelines

Safety in the Elementary (K–6) Science Classroom, 2nd Edition*

Foreword

Science education in the elementary school is crucial to the education of our children. Hands-on science activities encourage students to become active participants in learning about the world around them. This material is designed to assist elementary science teachers with one of the special aspects of teaching science, that of making the experimental environment safe for the students. As chair of the Committee on Chemical Safety of the American Chemical Society, I would like to thank the committee members who prepared the first edition of this publication in 1993, Jack Breazeale (who chaired the subcommittee), Robert Alaimo, Patricia Redden, Jay Young, Maureen Matkovich (ACS staff liaison), and, especially, Beverly DiMaio of the Horry County School District, South Carolina. Their hard work is gratefully acknowledged. This second edition contains updated references and graphics but essentially has the same text as the first edition.

Diane G. Schmidt, Chair, Committee on Chemical Safety, April 2001

Disclaimer

These materials have been compiled by recognized authorities from sources believed to be reliable and to represent the best opinions on the subject. This publication is intended to serve only as a starting point for good practices and does not purport to specify minimal legal standards or to represent the policy of the American Chemical society. No warranty, guarantee, or representation is made by the American Chemical Society as to the accuracy or sufficiency of the information contained herein, and the Society assumes no responsibility in connection therewith. This manual is intended to provide basic guidelines for safe practices. Therefore, it cannot be assumed that all necessary warning and precautionary measures are contained in this document and that other or additional information or measures may not be required. The American Chemical Society does not warrant that the recommendations contained in these materials meet or comply with the requirements of any safety code or regulation of any state, municipality, or other jurisdiction. Users of this publication should consult pertinent local, state, and federal laws and legal counsel before initiating any safety program.

Introduction

Science is safe as long as teachers and students are aware of potential hazards and take necessary and appropriate precautions and safety measures. If students can take responsibility for being safety conscious, they will be better prepared and better disciplined for the higher-level sciences.

Objectives of This Manual

1. To make teachers aware of the potential hazards that exist in an elementary science classroom.

2. To help teachers organize their classes so that injuries can be prevented.

3. To help teachers evaluate safety aspects of an experiment or science activity and become aware of hazards that may exist.

4. To make students aware of the importance of safety in the classroom.

Safety Through Organization

Many potential hazards can be eliminated if the teacher has an organized and disciplined classroom. To do this, the teacher needs to perform the experiment before assigning it to the students. Then, as a result of the prior performance, the teacher will be familiar with the activity, will have the materials ready to distribute to the students, will be ready to supervise the students' activities, will have a plan for collecting materials after the activity, and will be able to instruct the students in what is expected of them.

Helpful suggestions can be found in several resources. The teacher's edition of the textbook being used should have safety information on the activities. The state department of education should have publications available to assist with matters of safety and disposal. Many science supply houses offer safety and disposal publications. Expert advice can be obtained from organizations such as the American Chemical Society, the Laboratory Safety Institute, the National Association of Biology Teachers, and the National Science Teachers Association. If a college or university is nearby, members of the science faculty are usually willing to assist in safety matters. (Addresses and telephone numbers of the organizations listed above appear at the end of this publication.)

Eye and Personal Protection

1. Teachers should always wear chemical splash-proof safety goggles when working with chemicals, as should students working or watching in the area. Child-sized goggles are available from science materials suppliers.

2. Teachers and students should wear safety goggles whenever there is a possibility of flying objects or projectiles, such as when working with rubber bands.

3. Safety goggles used by more than one person should be sterilized between uses. One possible method of sterilization is to immerse the goggles in diluted laundry bleach followed by thorough rinsing and drying.

4. Proper precautions must be taken when using sharp objects such as knives, scalpels, compasses with sharp points, needles, and pins.

5. Students should not clean up broken glass. Teachers should use a broom and dustpan without touching the broken glass. Broken glass must be disposed of in a manner to prevent cuts or injury to the teacher, students, and custodial staff.

6. Teachers may decide to wear a laboratory apron or smock to prevent soiling or damage to clothing; if so, students should be similarly attired.

7. When working with hot materials, noxious plants, or live animals, teachers and students should wear appropriate hand protection.

8. Teachers and students should wash their hands upon completion of any experimental activity or at the end of the instructional session.

Safety With Fire and Heat Sources

1. Teachers should never leave the room while any flame is lighted or other heat source is in use.

2. Never heat flammable liquids. Heat only water or water solutions.

3. Use only glassware made from borosilicate glass (Kimax or Pyrex) for heating.

4. When working around a heat source, tie back long hair and secure loose clothing.

5. The area surrounding a heat source should be clean and have no combustible materials nearby.

6. When using a hot plate, locate it so that a child cannot pull it off the worktop or trip over the power cord.

7. Never leave the room while the hot plate is plugged in, whether or not it is in use; never allow students near an in-use hot plate if the teacher is not immediately beside the students.

8. Be certain that hot plates have been unplugged and are cool before handling. Check for residual heat by placing a few drops of water on the hot plate surface.

9. Never use alcohol burners.

10. Students should use candles only under the strict supervision of the teacher. Candles should be placed in a "drip pan" such as an aluminum pie plate large enough to contain the candle if it is knocked over.

11. The teacher should wear safety goggles and use heat-resistant mitts when working with hot materials. All students near hot liquids should wear safety goggles.

12. The teacher should keep a fire extinguisher near the activity area and be trained in its use.

13. The teacher should know what to do in case of fire. If a school policy does not exist, check with local fire officials for information.

Procedures for Using Dangerous Materials

1. Use only safety matches. Even safety matches should be used only with direct teacher supervision.

2. Use only nonmercury thermometers. Mercury from broken thermometers is difficult to clean up, and the vapors from spilled mercury are dangerous. Remember that thermometers are fragile; when students are handling them, supervise them so that the students won't use the thermometers as a stirring rod or allow them to roll off the table.

3. Store batteries with at least one terminal covered with tape. Batteries exhibiting any corrosion should be discarded. Because the contents of batteries are

potentially hazardous, batteries should not be cut open or taken apart. Check to see if batteries can be recycled in your area.

4. Never tell, encourage, or allow students to place any materials in or near their mouth, nose, or eyes.

5. Materials may include household chemicals. Before using household chemicals or other materials, study the label carefully to learn the hazards and precautions associated with such materials. Similarly, study the labels of chemicals purchased from a scientific supply house. The commercial suppliers of laboratory chemicals will furnish Material Safety Data Sheets (MSDSs) that describe the hazards and precautions for such materials in detail. These MSDSs should be on file in the school district office, and copies should be available in the classroom.

6. Do not touch "dry ice" (solid carbon dioxide) with the bare skin. Always wear cotton or insulated gloves when handling dry ice. Do not store or place dry ice in a sealed container.

7. Liquid spills can be slippery. Clean up any spill immediately and properly as soon as it occurs. Follow the cleanup instructions given on the label or the MSDS for the substance.

8. Do not mix or use chemicals in any manner other than that stated in the approved procedure. At no time should a teacher undertake a new procedure without prior and full investigation of the chemical and physical properties of the materials to be used and of the outcomes of the proposed procedures. When planning to undertake a new procedure, it is a good practice to consult with a professional who is familiar with any potential problems.

Safety With Plants

1. Wash hands after working with seeds and plants. Many store-bought seeds have been coated with insecticides and/or fertilizers.

2. Never put seeds or plants in the mouth.

3. Do not handle seeds or plants if there are cuts or sores on the hands.

4. Some 700 species of plants are known to cause death or illness. Be aware of plants in the local area that are harmful. For more information, contact the local county agricultural agent.

5. Be aware of the signs of plant poisoning and act quickly if a student exhibits such signs after a lesson. Symptoms may include one or more of the following: headache, nausea, dizziness, vomiting, skin eruption, itching, or other skin irritation.

6. Be particularly alert to plant safety on field trips.

Safety With Animals

1. All handling of animals by students must be done voluntarily and only under immediate teacher supervision.

2. Students should not be allowed to mishandle or mistreat animals.

3. A safety lesson should be given to teach the students how to care for and treat the animal. A safety lesson on proper care and treatment of the animal should be given to students, ideally before the animal is brought into the classroom.

4. Animals caught in the wild should not be brought into the classroom. For example, turtles are carriers of salmonella, and many wild animals are subject to rabies.

5. On field trips or during other outdoor activities, be aware of the danger of rabies exposure from wild animals. Also be aware of the potential hazards of insect bites, such as allergic reactions to bee stings or diseases spread by ticks or fleas.

6. At no time should dissection be done on an animal corpse unless it was specifically purchased for that purpose from a reliable supplier.

7. Any animal species that has been preserved in formaldehyde should not be used.

Emergency Procedures

1. Establish emergency procedures for at least the following: emergency first aid, electric shock, poisoning, burns, fire, evacuations, spills, and animal bites.

2. Evaluate each experimental procedure in advance of classroom use so that plans may be made in advance to handle possible emergencies.

3. Be sure that equipment and supplies needed for foreseen emergencies are available in or near the classroom.

4. Establish procedures for the notification of appropriate authorities and response agencies in the event of an emergency.

Disposal

Except for the disposal procedures described in the textbook in use, it is unlikely that any of the wastes generated in elementary science activities will be harmful to the environment. If the teacher has any questions concerning waste disposal, the science supervisor for the school or school district should be consulted.

Safety Awareness of Students

Safety instruction should begin at the earliest possible age. Students can begin to learn the importance of safety in the classroom, laboratory, and life in general at the elementary school level. The teacher must set the rules, but the teacher should also explain to the students why the rules are necessary. The students must also realize that anyone who does not follow the rules will lose the privilege of taking part in the fun, hands-on activities.

To reinforce the rules, teachers should engage the students in a discussion or activity. One activity could be a poster contest. The winning posters could be displayed in the room and used throughout the year to stress safety and enforce the safety rules.

General Safety Rules for Students

Always review the general safety rules with the students before beginning an activity.

1. Never do any experiment without the approval and direct supervision of your teacher.

2. Always wear your safety goggles when your teacher tells you to do so. Never remove your goggles during an activity.

3. Know the location of all safety equipment in or near your classroom. Never play with the safety equipment.

4. Tell your teacher immediately if an accident occurs.

5. Tell your teacher immediately if a spill occurs.

6. Tell your teacher immediately about any broken, chipped, or scratched glassware so that it may be properly cleaned up and disposed of.

7. Tie back long hair and secure loose clothing when working around flames.

8. If instructed to do so, wear your laboratory apron or smock to protect your clothing.

9. Never assume that anything that has been heated is cool. Hot glassware looks just like cool glassware

10. Never taste anything during a laboratory activity. If an investigation involves tasting, it will be done in the cafeteria.

11. Clean up your work area upon completion of your activity.

12. Wash your hands with soap and water upon completion of an activity.

Index

Index

Index